BLACK+DECKER

CUSTOM GRILLS & SMOKERS

Build Your Own Backyard Cooking & Tailgating Equipment

Brimming with creative inspiration, how-to projects, and useful information to enrich your everyday life, Quarto Knows is a favourite destination for those pursuing their interests and passions. Visit our site and dig deeper with our books into your area of interest: Quarto Creates, Quarto Cooks, Quarto Homes, Quarto Lives, Quarto Drives, Quarto Explores, Quarto Gifts, or Quarto Kids.

© 2017 Quarto Publishing Group USA Inc.

First published in 2017 by Cool Springs Press, an imprint of The Quarto Group, 401 Second Avenue North, Suite 310, Minneapolis, MN 55401 USA. T (612) 344-8100 F (612) 344-8692 www.QuartoKnows.com

All rights reserved. No part of this book may be reproduced in any form without written permission of the copyright owners. All images in this book have been reproduced with the knowledge and prior consent of the artists concerned, and no responsibility is accepted by producer, publisher, or printer for any infringement of copyright or otherwise, arising from the contents of this publication. Every effort has been made to ensure that credits accurately comply with information supplied. We apologize for any inaccuracies that may have occurred and will resolve inaccurate or missing information in a subsequent reprinting of the book.

Cool Springs Press titles are also available at discount for retail, wholesale, promotional, and bulk purchase. For details, contact the Special Sales Manager by email at specialsales@quarto.com or by mail at The Quarto Group, Attn: Special Sales Manager, 401 Second Avenue North, Suite 310, Minneapolis, MN 55401 USA.

10 9 8 7 6 5 4 3 2 1

ISBN: 978-0-7603-5354-7

Library of Congress Cataloging-in-Publication Data
Names: Cool Springs Press, issuing body. | Black & Decker Corporation (Towson, Md.), contributor.
Title: Black & Decker custom grills & smokers : build your own backyard cooking & tailgating equipment / by editors of Cool Springs Press.
Other titles: Black and Decker custom grills and smokers
Description: Minneapolis, Minnesota : Cool Springs Press, [2017] | Includes bibliographical references and index.
Identifiers: LCCN 2017030791 | ISBN 9780760353547 (pb)
Subjects: LCSH: Outdoor cooking. | Barbecues (Fireplaces) | Gas grills.
Classification: LCC TX840.B3 B5566 2017 | DDC 641.5/78--dc23
LC record available at https://lccn.loc.gov/2017030791

Acquiring Editor: Mark Johanson
Project Manager: Jordan Wiklund
Art Director: James Kegley
Layout: Danielle Smith-Boldt
Photography: Paul Markert
Photo Assistance: Brad Holden, Ian Miller

Printed in China

Custom Grills & Smokers: Build Your Own Backyard Cooking & Tailgating Equipment
Created by: The Editors of Cool Springs Press, in cooperation with BLACK+DECKER.
BLACK+DECKER and the BLACK+DECKER logo are trademarks of The Black & Decker Corporation and are used under license. All rights reserved.

NOTICE TO READERS

For safety, use caution, care, and good judgment when following the procedures described in this book. The publisher and BLACK+DECKER cannot assume responsibility for any damage to property or injury to persons as a result of misuse of the information provided.

The techniques shown in this book are general techniques for various applications. In some instances, additional techniques not shown in this book may be required. Always follow manufacturers' instructions included with products, since deviating from the directions may void warranties. The projects in this book vary widely as to skill levels required: some may not be appropriate for all do-it-yourselfers, and some may require professional help.

Consult your local building department for information on building permits, codes, and other laws as they apply to your project.

Contents

Custom Grills & Smokers

Contents (Cont.)

Introduction

Few summer pleasures rival cooking and eating outside. Whether you're just throwing together a simple burgers-and-hot-dogs backyard cookout, or planning a full-blown smoker session to prepare delectable brisket for twenty of your closest friends, you're part of an American tradition. Even the early colonists had the cookout bug, capturing wild pigs and slowly roasting the beasts on spits over pits filled with applewood coals.

Food cooked out in the open just tastes better. A quick-seared chicken breast beats an oven-broiled version hands-down. And a pork shoulder smoked to fall-apart perfection? There's just no comparison with anything that comes out of a kitchen. The only way to make those outdoor flavors even better is to prepare the food in a cooker you crafted yourself. Sure, you could be like all the other people on your block and buy a nice shiny grill or plunk down a small fortune for the latest trendy smoker. But why? Why spend your hard-earned cash on something that is really quite simple to build? The truth is, constructing a grill, smoker, or even a true barbecue oven is a fairly basic DIY project. These structures are generally forgiving of small imperfections, and the use you'll get out of a homemade smokehouse or brick pizza oven will more than repay you for the time and effort invested.

Outdoor cooking structures come in all sizes, shapes, materials, and capacities. Familiar with basic masonry techniques? How about building a brick barbecue (page 102) as a handsome addition to your backyard, and one that will give you decades of delicious service? Prefer a project that's a bit more modest? Why not tackle a simple barrel grill (page 96), an ideal way to recycle a used container into a long-lasting cooker? And all that just scratches the surface. Leaf through this book and you'll find instructions for cookout accessories, pizza ovens, complete outdoor kitchens, and more.

Of course, sometimes you want to cook on the go, putting together a delicious feast in the parking lot outside the biggest game of the year. That's why *BLACK+DECKER Custom Grills & Smokers* also covers tailgating. That section includes intriguing and useful projects, from a smoker you can bring with you to the game (page 140) to a pub cooler (page 164) that will keep your liquid refreshments perfectly chilled.

The truth is, if there's a way to cook something outdoors, you'll find it in this book. Choose a project that suits your cookout style and preferences, plan for where you'll put it, and then get to work. Summer's not going to last forever, and you want to enjoy every last bite of it.

Custom Cooker Gallery

Size a simple smoker to accommodate what you're most likely to smoke. This barrel smoker allows for two briskets at a time—more than enough to feed a large crowd and have plenty of leftovers.

Put basic metalworking skills to work in crafting a simple backyard grill for easy and quick cookouts. A fundamental cookout unit like this takes very little time, expertise, or energy to throw together and it works just as well as a store-bought model would. The capacity is limited, but for modest cookouts, this will more than do the trick.

Create a basic smoker from nothing more than a drum, a couple pieces of rebar, and an extra drum lid. At its heart, smoking meat just requires a consistent low temperature, with a fuel source producing smoke that is trapped with whatever you're smoking. So making the bottom of a drum a fire chamber and the top a smoker box can be easy as pie. Just make sure that the drum is scrupulously clean.

Slice a barrel in half lengthwise to make a handy grill with plenty of cooking area. The length of a halved barrel allows for multiple heat areas, and the structure can comfortably sit on many different supports, including a table base like the one used here.

Ensure success in an outdoor brick oven by building in removable, adjustable grates. Adjustability allows you to cook different foods, or different cuts, to perfection. It also enables you to accommodate different woods and fuel sources burning at different temperatures.

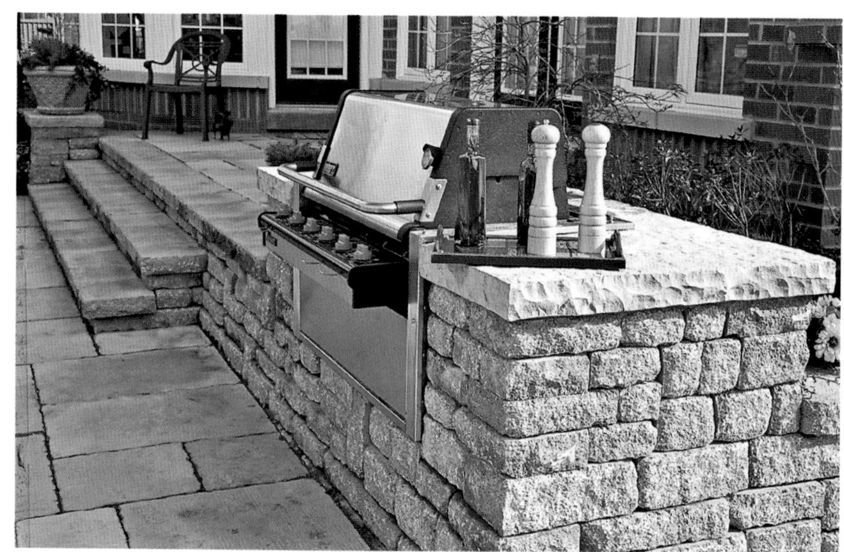

Combine the convenience and control of a manufactured grill with the customization of a DIY project by incorporating a "drop-in" grill unit into a masonry wall or outdoor kitchen surface. The simple structure of stacked stone in this yard supports a fully functional gas grill, leaving more than enough room for whatever the chef might want to cook.

Go fancy with a built-in, wood-fired brick oven. An outdoor structure like this can be built right into a stucco wall of a patio and is the perfect cooking cavity for delicious pizza and breads.

Mount a barrel smoker on wheels and you can have true barbecue at your next tailgating party. This tow-behind rig can be fired up hours before you're ready to leave for the game (depending on what you're smoking) and then brought along to provide an authentic feast for friends and other fans.

Use a moveable screen for maximum control. This homemade tray grill provides plenty of room for different heating areas, but rather than move the meat, a sliding grill allows the cook to just slide it to a cooler or hotter part of the grill.

Build a luxury garden feature in the form of an outdoor oven with a separate firebox. A structure like this takes expertise and expense to build, but will easily last as long as your house, and the oven will just get better with age.

Match the outdoor oven to your home and skill level. A simple wood-fired oven tower like this one can be fairly easy for the home DIYer because the design is based on straight lines and is fairly forgiving. It's also a modest size that won't take forever to construct. The cavity beneath the oven leaves plenty of room for firewood, and the entire unit needs only a modest corner of the patio.

Create a patio centerpiece out of a wood-fired oven. Whether you have the masonry skills or need to hire help to build an oven like this, it can easily be ground zero for all your outdoor entertaining. Cover it with a patio roof like the one shown here and you can even use the oven to cook pizza in the winter.

Bring the barbecue to your next campout. A portable smoker like this one is ideal for a long-term campground where you want to enjoy the taste of smoked meat, fish, or poultry. Vent holes in the bottom allow the smoke to fill the interior, and the unit can be set up wherever you can lay a bed of flaming logs.

Make it easy with a grill basket. Grill baskets come in many forms, from perforated trays to handled containers like the basket shown here, but they all allow you to grill smaller, or less solid, items. Choose a handled basket and whatever you cook will be easy to flip and control.

Press your fire pit into double duty. All you need to turn a fire pit into a grill is a grate that fits neatly on top. The simple fire pit here was formed of interlocking curved pavers, but just about any patio fire pit can serve as a simple grill for cooking dogs or burgers.

Build large if you plan on cooking ahead. One of the great things about smoked barbecue meat is that it can keep. Build a large smoker like this brick structure and you can smoke a lot of meat at one time—a great way to take advantage of meat on sale.

Add a glorious visual to your yard by building a true fieldstone smokehouse. Smoke your food year-round in a structure such as this, which is a handsome fixture in the yard and the sign of a serious barbecuer.

Apply your woodworking skills to build a smokebox. A simple construction like this cedar unit can be a great home smoking option and won't tax your woodworking skills. It's also an attractive look that will weather well and add a nice visual wherever you place it.

Combine a smoker box with a homemade grill for a dynamic duo that can handle any task. This crude box grill is great for grilling anything from ribs to burgers, but it can also serve as the firebox for a box smoker. The smoker is simply placed on top of the grill to create an easy-to-maintain smoking operation that will yield perfectly smoked meat.

Smoke the day's catch with a handy portable smoke box. Caught more fish than you can eat on your camping trip? No worries—smoke the extra in a simple box like this one. A crude grill holds the box out of the fire, and a perforated bottom allows the smoke to saturate the interior of the box and the fish.

Get your grilling off to a perfect start. A coal-starter chimney like this one can be bought or just as easily made. Either way, it's just about an essential accessory for any outdoor griller looking to lay down a bed of hot coals as quickly and efficiently as possible.

Skewer your grilled goods for optimal control. Your homemade grill doesn't necessarily need grates. A set of skewers are perfect for grilling small hunks of meat, kebobs, various vegetables, and smaller proteins like prawns.

Make perfect pizza. Although it can seem a significant investment in time and effort, build an outdoor pizza oven and you may be shocked at how much use you get out of it. Not only does an oven like this one create incomparable pizza crust, you can use it to bake delectable breads and even traditional picnic dishes like casseroles.

Stylize your outdoor oven to match the look of your yard and home. Just because it's a functional cooking structure, there's still no excuse not to put your own signature touches on an outdoor oven. The brick showpiece in this yard includes a stone roof, concrete counter, and plenty of room for the requisite firewood—all in a very attractive structure.

Use your ingenuity to find a grill just about anywhere. The simple grill on the left is the ultimate in recycling—it's a retired toolbox. The simple quick campground grill on the right is an old car wheel. These prove that grills can be just about any metal structure with a cavity for coals and an opening over which to roast your dinner.

Plan for size. If you throw big cookout parties with scores of extended family and friends, or if you like to barbecue large cuts of beef or pork, it only makes sense to build a grill big enough to handle everything. These side-by-side stone-and-brick monsters are capable of handling a forty-person cookout or just about a complete pig. Building both at the same time meant the project wasn't much harder than building one.

GRILLING & SMOKING BASICS

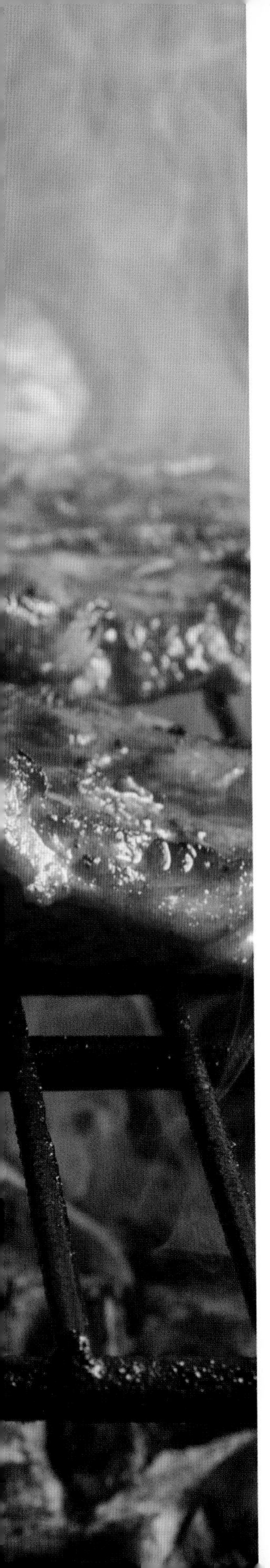

Cook with Confidence

Cooking a meal outdoors can seem exceedingly simple, but success depends on managing many variables. Construct your own cooker and you take control over the process from the start. Rather than trying to make the force fit between what's available at retail and the type of cooking you want to do, you have the chance to design a cooking chamber that is exactly the size you want it to be, with space for the fuel source you prefer and the controls you'll find most useful. Of course, along the way you'll be saving a good deal of money.

But even before you start, you'll have to make some cooking decisions. Are you looking to grill small cuts rapidly over high heat? If so, you can make do with a simpler structure, incorporating a fixed or adjustable grill directly over where the fuel source will lay. But maybe you're a fan of traditional "low-and-slow" barbecuing, cooking larger cuts for long periods of time over temperatures as low as 200 degrees Fahrenheit. In that case, you'll need a larger space for the fuel source with separate access (to feed the fire over long cooking sessions), and grates capable of supporting heavier loads. Or perhaps you're all about smoking meat (even lower temperatures and longer cooking periods). If that's your preference, you'll need a completely separate firebox with a proper air-movement design to feed smoke into a tightly enclosed cooking chamber (and a way to vent the smoke).

The decisions don't end once you've built your cooker. Fuel sources vary. Maintaining any cooker's heat source can be tricky, especially when you need to keep the temperature steady over long periods of time. Different types of cooking make different demands on the cook.

All those basics are what this section is about. Consider this the foundation of knowledge you need to cook exactly the food you want to eat, with a minimum of fuss, wasted effort, or burned meat. Understanding all the variables is the first step in building a cooker that will serve you for years, and help you make delectable, unforgettable meals.

Why Build Your Own Cooker?

If you're into cooking with fire, you probably already know that customization is big part of the fun, whether you're concocting your own special blend of fuels, perfecting a new cooking method, or modifying your equipment to fine-tune its performance. And building your own cooker is the ultimate in customization. It's true to the creative and primal traditions of cooking outdoors, and it teaches you about the relationship between fire and food. It also can save you a lot of money and perhaps let you try some cooking methods you otherwise might not venture into due to the high cost of new equipment.

Custom cookers have always been integral to cooking with fire and smoke.

On the other hand, if you're new to grilling or smoking, building your own cooker is the ideal way to start, for all of the reasons mentioned above.

Tradition

Grilling and smoking are deeply rooted in traditions of invention and innovation. The barbecue masters of the old days used the equipment, animals, and wood fuel they could gather nearby. They performed their magic in cinder block pits and tin smoke shacks, making modifications as they learned from experience and tweaking their equipment and technique to suit their own style. In fact, a lot of barbecue masters today do exactly the same thing. Building your own custom cooker follows that longstanding tradition and brings you a little closer to the essence of cooking with fire.

Cost

Buying outdoor cooking equipment—good equipment—can require a significant investment. It seems to be one of those categories of products that automatically comes with an extra markup. You can find inexpensive versions of most kinds of grills and some types of smokers, but you usually get what you pay for. When an offset smoker comes in a box of parts, and you can easily carry it inside by yourself, you know it's not going to last very long. Building your own equipment saves you a lot of money because you're using ordinary building materials without the extra markup (and, of course, your labor is free). This goes double for pizza ovens, which, when bought at a store can literally cost as much as a trip to Italy.

Customization

Building your own cooker lets you customize your setup in many ways, from the mechanics of the design to the decorative touches. You can choose the size, the materials, and the configuration as you like. You can add a grate here, a vent there. When you've built a cooker from scratch, you get a better understanding of how it works and can make adjustments and modifications over time. With this in mind, it's easy to understand why there are so many homemade grills and smokers out there. For a lot of serious outdoor cooks, the cookers themselves become a hobby and a source of pride, almost as much as the food they turn out.

Put your mark on your project with personal touches or custom design features.

Grilling Methods & Equipment

Since grilling is something that's done in almost every backyard and in almost every culture throughout the world, grilling itself doesn't need much of an introduction. But what might be less familiar are the differences between grilling and smoking or other types of outdoor cooking. The main differences are temperature and proximity to the fire. Grilling is done with a hotter fire and with the food much closer to the fire than with smoking. This also usually translates to a much faster cooking process.

There are many sizes, shapes, and types of grills, and nearly as many ways to categorize them all. An easy way to choose your equipment is to consider where you will use the grill and for what type of cooking. If you're primarily into grilling but want to try smoking, or you just don't have a smoker yet, there are a few easy ways to bring extra smoke to your grill; see **Smoking on a Grill** on page 26.

Outdoor ovens—both traditional and custom—are made with humble materials, like brick, mortar, and concrete.

Conventional Grilling

Conventional grilling is cooking on a grate over a charcoal or gas fire. Conventional grills include all of the standard backyard or patio varieties, such as kettle grills and rectangular gas grills, plus traditional brick barbecues on the large end of the spectrum, and simple portable grills on the small end. For custom designs, it's hard to beat a simple barrel grill made with a repurposed steel barrel. This works as well as most store-bought grills and offers a great deal of cooking capacity.

Because they're easy to fire up and are often used for everyday meals, conventional grills may be seen as an extension of the home's kitchen. And that's probably why conventional grills are the centerpiece of so many outdoor kitchens.

Conventional grills typically have two grates, one for cooking and one for holding the coals. The coal grate allows air to flow beneath and up through the coals. This is essential for fast starting and for maintaining a hot fire. The grate also allows ashes to fall to the bottom of the grill so they don't smother the burning coals.

Another key feature of a grill is the lid, for those that have them. Grills that don't have lids are sometimes called *open* grills. These are ideal for hot fires and quick cooking—things like steak, vegetables, satay, and seafood. Grills with lids are covered grills. With the cover off, grills with lids work just like open grills, but having a lid makes a covered grill much more versatile. Covering a grill gives you more control over the fire, and it allows for lower temperatures and slower cooking. Grills are usually covered for indirect cooking (see **Direct and Indirect Heat** on page 24) and always for smoking on a grill.

DIRECT AND INDIRECT HEAT

Generally speaking, there are two basic methods of cooking on a grill: *direct* and *indirect*. Direct heating is placing the food directly over the fire. The hot coals usually are spread evenly over the entire coal grate to deliver even, intense heat straight upward to the cooking grate. Direct heat is used for fast cooking of relatively small or tender foods: burgers, steaks, sauté, vegetables, and most seafood. These are foods that can cook sufficiently on the inside in the time it takes to give the outside a nice char.

Indirect heating involves moving the coals to one or both sides of the grill and placing the food in the center of the cooking grate so it is not directly above any coals. The most intense heat moves *around* the food, cooking it more gradually. This is how you cook whole chickens and other large pieces of meat, like butts, roasts, and ribs. These foods require lower, slower heat to cook internally and tenderize over time. Cooking them with direct heat would produce an overcooked outside and undercooked inside.

Sometimes it's best to use both methods, starting with direct heat to sear or char the exterior, then moving the coals and cooking the rest of the way with indirect heat. Taking a different approach, when you're smoking on a grill, the heat is always indirect.

Direct heat is for fast, hot grilling.

For indirect heat, coals can simply be pushed to either side, or they can be corralled in a charcoal basket.

A barrel grill (above) and kettle grill are classic conventional grills that use charcoal or wood. Both have covers and work well for direct and indirect heating.

Brick barbecues are large open grills ideal for "cookout" foods, like burgers, steaks, and kebabs.

Open-Fire Grilling

Open-fire grilling is cooking over or in front of an open fire. You can do it with any campfire and open-fire grilling is ideal for a backyard fire pit. It can require a lot of attention to both the fire and the food, but it's a primal and social method of cooking that's perfect for friendly gatherings and outdoor events.

Depending on the equipment you bring to the fire, open-fire cooking can be just like grilling, with either direct or indirect heat, or it can be a much slower process, such as roasting. Conventional grilling simply requires a grill grate supported over the fire. Roasting requires a rotisserie setup. There are also many other traditional methods of cooking over an open fire, such as with a Dutch oven or a cowboy grill. When building your own outdoor fire pit, you can design it for the type of cooking you'll do most as well as for how you'll use the pit when you're not cooking.

Tailgating

Cooking with fire is an essential part of tailgating, and for most tailgaters that means grilling. Tailgating grills tend to be relatively small and highly portable, for easy transport. They're also easy to set up and break down. The same is true for tailgating accessories, like prep tables, coolers, and places to eat and drink. You want your setup to be efficient, comfortable, and welcoming; you just don't want to spend a lot of time getting set up.

Cooking equipment for tailgating includes open grills, covered grills, and even portable smokers. The **Tailgate Smoker** project on page 140 is a small covered grill that you convert to a smoker with the addition of a large steamer pot. It's small enough to fit into any tailgating setup, and if you decide to grill instead of smoke, simply leave out the pot.

Lightweight and road-ready is the name of the game for tailgating equipment.

Smoking Methods & Equipment

Smokers come in even more varieties than grills. On top of that, many grills can be used as smokers, giving you still more options. Perhaps the best way to narrow the choices is to consider the type of smoking you'd like to do most. Smoking methods can generally be grouped by the temperature ranges used during the smoking process. Some smokers are suitable for all temperatures, while others are best suited to one temperature range or method of smoking.

Rotisserie cooking over an open fire uses radiant heat from the fire to slowly roast the food.

Smoking Temperatures: Cold, Warm, and Hot

Most smoking is done at temperatures between 65° and 300°F. To put that into perspective, conventional grilling is done at about 400° to 600°F, and cooking in an outdoor oven usually starts at about 750°F. The range of smoking temperatures can be broken down into three categories: cold, warm, and hot.

Cold smoking temperatures range from about 65° to 100°F, and is usually somewhere in the 80° range. When you consider that this is no hotter than a mild summer day, you realize that cold smoking is mostly about smoke and not much heat. It imparts a mild smoke flavor without cooking the food. This is used for very slow smoking of salmon (and other fish) and ham as well as for quicker smoke-flavoring of things like cheese, salt, nuts, fruits, and any other foods that would do well with a hint of smoke. Curing foods like salmon and ham with this process takes a lot of time and expertise, and most home smokers aren't suitable for days of smoking at such low temperatures.

Warm smoking temperatures range between 150° and 175°F. Right in the middle of this range is the sweet spot for making jerky, which is dehydrated and cured (with the help of salt) as it's smoked. This is a great smoking method for beginners because it's hard to get wrong and the results are fantastic. Homemade beef jerky is a different world from store-bought, and homemade salmon jerky is out of this world. Warm

SMOKING ON A GRILL

Can you really smoke food in a conventional grill? Yes, but your options are somewhat limited. You can certainly add plenty of smoke to grilled food, by simply adding wood chunks or chips to an existing charcoal fire (or even gas heat). And you can keep the fire low and use the indirect cooking method (see **Direct and Indirect Heat** on page 24) to slow-cook chicken and large cuts of beef or pork, again while adding smoke. But true barbecue, which requires a temperature between 225° and 275°F sustained for many hours, can be challenging on a grill and might not be worth the trouble. In most cases, the food is just too close to the heat for classic "low and slow" smoking.

There are a few easy ways to introduce wood smoke to grilled food, whether you're using a charcoal or gas grill (see **Fuel Sources** on page 31 for more information on wood chips and chunks):

Smoker box: A smoker box is a metal box with a perforated lid. Some are rectangular, some are curved (to fit along the inside of a round kettle grill), and some have V-shaped bottoms (to fit between the flame deflector bars of a gas grill). Simply fill the box with wood chips or small chunks and set it onto the grill directly over the heat source. The wood pieces will smolder and smoke. Replenish the chips or chunks as the burnt pieces turn to ash. A cold smoker (or smoke generator) is a similar device that can work on top of a grill grate; see **Cold Smokers** on page 28.

Wood chip pouch: Add 1–2 cups of dry or soaked and drained wood chips to a large piece of aluminum foil. Fold the foil over the chips and enclose the ends to form a completely enclosed pouch. (Some people like to fold in the ends and roll it up like a burrito.) Poke a dozen or so holes in the top of the pouch, using a skewer or the tip of a knife. Place the pouch onto the grill's cooking grate, directly over the heat. Or, you can nestle the pouch directly into or under the hot coals or place it directly onto the burner of a gas grill. If you're using a gas grill, heat it on HIGH until the pouch begins to smoke, then turn down the heat. When grilling with indirect heat, use a pouch at each end (wherever the heat is). You can also buy a reusable metal mesh pouches that works just like a homemade version, only better.

Wood chunks: Place a few large wood chunks onto burning coals of a charcoal grill or directly onto the briquettes or heat diffuser bars of a gas grill. Let the wood smolder and burn while you cook. This is a good technique for adding smoke while you're grilling, rather than slow-cooking or smoking. If the chunks flare up, spray the flames with a mist from a water bottle; it's best not to let flames touch the food.

smoking can also be used to smoke—and precook—large cuts of meat, like ribs, butts, shoulders, and roasts. Once these are smoked for a while, they must be fully cooked in an oven or grill. Warm smoking also can do a lot of what a cold smoker does but in a shorter time. For example, if you want to smoke cheese or nuts and your smoker just gets too hot for true cold smoking, you can warm-smoke the food and take it off before much cooking occurs.

Hot smoking temperatures range between 200° and 300°F. This is the realm of classic American *barbecue*, which is typically smoked between 225° and 275°F. The key difference between warm smoking and hot smoking is that hot smoking methods typically cook the food completely. In addition to preparing favorites like ribs, brisket, and pulled pork, hot smoking can be used for whole chickens and even whole hogs. Most barrel- and kettle-type smokers are designed for hot smoking (but can be used for lower-temperature smoking). Any smoking done on a conventional charcoal or gas grill is likely to be hot smoking, given the proximity of the food to the fire.

Types of Smokers (including tailgating/small smokers)

Despite the wide range of smoker designs, all smokers have many of the same essential parts:

- A place for the fire: may be a separate chamber or simply an elevated grate for the coals or a smoker box for holding smoldering wood chips or other fuel
- A place for the food: usually a cooking grate or hanging rack; always located higher than the fire so that smoke naturally rises up and around the food
- Vents: for fueling the fire with oxygen, creating circulation for smoke, and controlling the temperature inside the smoker; more airflow means a hotter fire and higher cooking temperature

In addition, some smokers include a heat diffuser of some kind. This may be as simple as a metal sheet or a shallow bowl full of water. A heat diffuser is located between the fire and the food and deflects or diverts some of the fire's heat so it doesn't reach the food directly.

In the **Double-Barrel Smoker** (page 60), the baffle plate serves as both a heat diffuser and a barrier that creates a smoke channel. In the **Tailgate Smoker** (page 140), the bottom of the steamer pot serves as a heat diffuser and has holes that allow for airflow.

Double-Barrel Smoker

The classic backyard barbecue rig, a double-barrel smoker (also called an *offset* smoker) is characterized by its two chambers: a burning chamber, or *firebox*, and a cooking chamber, or *smoke chamber*. The firebox may hang off the side of the smoke chamber or it may be below. Separating the firebox allows you to keep a relatively hot fire while maintaining a relatively low, even temperature inside the smoke chamber. A standard offset smoker has a chimney on the opposite side of the smoke chamber from the firebox. This draws the smoke from the firebox over the food on its way to the chimney. An alternative design, sometimes called *reverse-flow*, has a chimney on the same side as the firebox (or the opening between the firebox and the smoke chamber). This draws the smoke and some of the heat underneath the food before it brings it back across the upper area of the smoke chamber.

Double-barrel smokers are also called "stick burners" because they are designed specifically for burning wood or charcoal. They are primarily used for traditional barbecue and other foods prepared with hot smoking. They can also be used for warm smoking if the fire is kept very small.

Double-barrel smokers have some similarities with conventional grills but include a separate firebox and a chimney.

The Double-Barrel Smoker (page 60) is a two-barrel design with a firebox (the lower barrel) underneath the smoke chamber (upper barrel).

Smokehouse & Other Warm/Cold Smokers

A smokehouse is a traditional smoking outfit with a history of producing smoked sausage, Virginia ham, smoked fish and cheeses, Scotch whiskey, and many other artisanal foods. As impressive as it may look in your backyard, a smokehouse is little more than a tiny shed or outdoor closet with shelves or racks for holding the food and an area at the bottom for the fire. And unless the bottom is made of solid masonry, the "fire" in this case is probably a smoker box with smoldering sawdust or pellets or an electric burner heating up a pan of wood chips.

The best thing about a smokehouse (apart from how cool it looks and how fun it is to use) is the large capacity. Even a small version can include four or five shelves, all of which you can fill for a single smoking. A smokehouse like this, with the fire inside the structure, is suitable for warm smoking and some cold smoking only. Burning a fire large and hot enough for hot smoking would likely turn the smokehouse into a house fire.

A backyard smokehouse makes a great conversation piece and is ideal for all kinds of warm-smoked foods. It is similar in function to a basic metal-box smoker.

COLD SMOKERS

Cold smokers, also called smoke generators, are perforated metal containers that hold wood pellets, chips, or sawdust. Once the fuel is ignited (a small propane torch works best), it smolders on its own until all of it is completely burned, leaving tidy piles of ash inside the smoker container. These smokers are handy for adding smoke when grilling or smoking with heat, but they're really designed for cold and warm smoking, where they are the sole source of heat and smoke.

Cold smokers can burn a full load of fuel from one to ten hours, depending on the size and design of the smoker, the fuel, and the temperature of the interior of the cooker. With many designs, you can burn the fuel starting at only one end (called a *single burn*) or from both ends (called a *double burn*). A double burn creates about twice as much smoke and heat and lasts about half as long as a single burn.

Cold smokers come in a variety of styles, including cylindrical and square tubes, maze-like trays, discs, and even hanging baskets similar to incense burners. These smokers are available from A-Maze-N (www.amazenproducts.com).

Cylindrical tube smoker.

Maze smoker for pellets.

If you've ever used a basic electric smoker—the kind consisting of a metal box with some wire racks inside, and heated with an electric burner—you have an idea of what you can do with a small backyard smokehouse, just on a bigger scale. Essentially, it's a big *warm smoker*. By contrast, many traditional smokehouses are designed with the fire or smoke source separated from the smokehouse itself, and the smoke is channeled into the food area via a flue or duct. This allows for much cooler temperatures and true cold smoking for foods like smoked salmon orham.

Upright Barrel Smokers

An upright barrel smoker is just what it sounds like; it's a steel barrel or cylinder set on its end, with a fire in the bottom and the food at the top. The smoke and heat go straight up and are controlled by vents near the bottom and top of the barrel. As simple as their design is, upright barrels are uncommonly versatile. Most can double as grills as well as smokers, and because they're assembled in a few pieces and are relatively small and lightweight, they're generally considered portable. Inside the barrel, most smokers can accommodate two grill racks, which provides extra cooking area as well as additional temperature control.

Upright barrels and similar cylindrical smokers are typically best suited to hot smoking at 225° to 300°F. Small barrel smokers are ideal for tailgating and for cooking at home when you don't have a lot of space, and this is where the two-in-one grill-smoker feature really comes in handy. At the other end of the size range, large smokers (often made with 30- or 55-gallon steel drums), can accommodate hanging the food from bars set across the top of the barrel. This is a popular method for smoking full racks ribs and whole turkeys.

One variation of the upright barrel is the water smoker, which has a rack or shelf directly above the fire that holds a shallow water pan. Filled with about two inches of water during most smoking processes, the water pan adds moisture to the air and serves as a heat deflector to prevent drying out or overheating the food. It can also be removed for crisping things like chicken skin. If you have a standard upright barrel smoker, you can experiment with using water by adding a pie pan filled water to a lower shelf.

The Tailgate Smoker (page 140) has an upright-barrel design and can be made with one or two racks for smoking. Removing the center "barrel" turns the smoker into a standard covered grill.

TIP

Hanging the food inside a tall upright barrel significantly increases the cooking capacity (when making ribs) and provides even smoke and heat (especially helpful for turkey).

The Clay Pot Smoker (page 42) is a fun-to-build variation using a couple of terra cotta planter pots. You don't need a barrel (or a grill) to have an upright smoker.

Cooking with Outdoor Ovens

If you've wondered what the hubbub around pizza ovens is all about, imagine this: for your whole life, every steak you'd ever eaten was cooked on a broiler pan in a conventional oven. Then one day you're invited to a barbecue and your host serves you a sizzling steak right off a charcoal grill. The meat is juicy and infused with wood smoke. It has burn marks and bits of char with intense caramelized flavors. There's variety from one bite to the next. Your steak never had these things before because it was cooked with electric heat, not a wood fire. A wood-fired oven does the same thing for pizza. The smoke, the char, the variety—you simply can't get these qualities with a conventional oven.

Pizza ovens are cousins to traditional stone or masonry bread ovens. The magic to their cooking quality comes from the deep, even heat retained in the brick floor and oven dome, and in the hint of wood smoke from the fire. It's not a strong smoke flavor because most of the smoke goes up through the chimney, but it adds a complexity and flavor profile that you can't get with any other method of cooking. The radiant heat from the fire provides another dimension to the cooking, allowing you to char foods by briefly facing them to the heat.

To cook in an outdoor oven, you start the fire in the center of the oven floor, which is made of high-temperature fire brick. As the fire burns, the entire oven heats up. The dome gets the hottest because

A brick oven with a barrel-shaped dome follows traditional Italian oven designs and is the easiest masonry oven to build.

Dome-style pizza ovens can be purchased as kits that you assemble on a new or existing concrete slab or a custom-built masonry base.

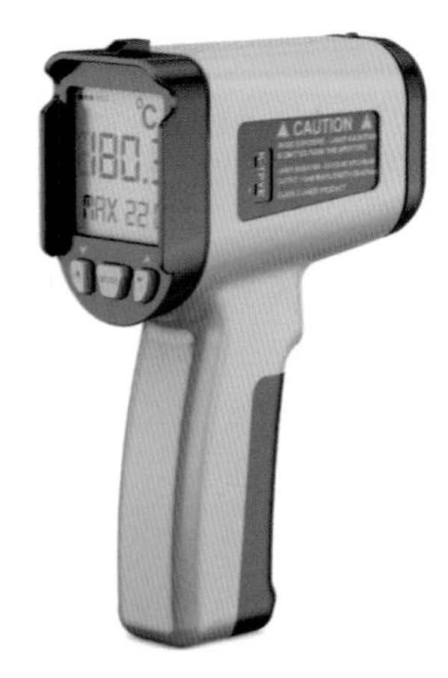

Infrared thermometers are widely available for under $50 and provide accurate (and safe) readings of the temperatures anywhere inside an oven.

Fire is control. Adjusting the oven temperature and the size and position of the fire and coals are the keys to an oven's versatility. Mastering this comes with experience, and that's half the fun of cooking with fire.

it's directly above the fire, but the floor is where you monitor the temperature. For pizza, the floor should be about 700° to 800°F. (measured with an infrared thermometer, not your hand). When the floor reaches the target temperature, you push the fire to one side of the oven and cook directly on the brick floor. Direct contact with the fire brick creates a crisp, perfectly charred crust, while the radiant heat of the dome cooks the top of the pizza. The more intense heat of the fire can bubble and blacken the edges of the crust as much as you like; this is why pizza cooks rotate the pizza and move it closer or farther away from the fire.

Of course, outdoor ovens can cook a lot more than pizza. They're great for bread and many kinds of meats, seafood, and vegetables. You can cook directly on the oven floor, as with pizza, or you can bake, roast, casserole, fry, or even grill food, with the use of an appropriate pan, crock, or grate. The trick to cooking any other food is to control the temperature. Since the oven takes a while to heat up, it makes sense to cook more than one thing with each firing. For example, you can roast vegetables or whole garlic bulbs while the oven is heating up, cook pizzas when the heat is at its peak, then bake some bread or a dessert as the fire and is dying down.

Fuel Sources

Once you have the decisions about equipment out of the way, the next big question is what kind of fuel you'll use to burn in that equipment. This seems like a critical call, and there's no shortage of opinions on the matter, but the fact is, it's no big deal, for a couple of reasons. First, as long as you choose decent-quality fuel sources and avoid the obvious pitfalls, like green wood or dumping match-lightable charcoal on the fire, you can't go too wrong. And second, you can always try something else, even during a single burn. That is, it's fine to throw on a different type of wood or charcoal, and you can always add wood to a charcoal fire that needs more smoke. In any case, experimentation is the name of the game. Once you get started, it won't be long before your own opinions are adding fuel to the fire.

Forms of Wood Fuel

Wood can play different roles for different types of outdoor cooking. For most backyard grilling and smoking, wood is used as a secondary fuel, primarily to add flavorful and aromatic smoke to a charcoal fire. This is because charcoal is easier to burn in the relatively small equipment used by home cooks, and it requires less tending. Also, many smokers and grills simply aren't designed for wood-only fires. However, there are a few notable exceptions: cold smoking and warm smoking typically are done with wood chips or sawdust, technically making these wood-only fires. Most offset smokers can handle wood fires and work just as well with charcoal. Cooking in ovens typically is done with just wood. Open-fire grilling in a fire pit can use any type of fire—logs, charcoal, scrap wood, stumps, whatever.

A combination of charcoal and wood is the main source for most grilling and smoking. Together, they often provide the ideal amounts of heat and smoke.

Logs

Small- to medium-size split logs are suitable for outdoor ovens and some offset smokers, while hefty campfire logs are best for fire pits and other open-fire cookers. Regardless of the size, there are a few basic rules to follow when choosing and using logs for cooking:

- **Hardwood:** With some exceptions for specialty smoked foods (like cedar-plank salmon), stick with hardwood for cooking with wood. Generally that means wood from deciduous trees rather than evergreen trees. Common softwoods like pine, cedar, and spruce have too much sap and emit a sooty smoke with off flavors. See **A Quick Guide to Wood Types** on page 34 for basic characteristics of common hardwoods.

- **Split wood:** Split wood starts more easily and burns more evenly than whole logs. It's also more

Split, well-seasoned hardwood logs are ideal for smokers, ovens, and fire pits.

likely to be properly seasoned (see below). It's fine if your logs have bark on them, but don't burn a pile of bark for a fire because it smokes too much and can add a bitter flavor.

- **Seasoned or kiln-dried:** Your wood must be dry. Seasoned wood is best. This has been split and dried in the open air for at least six months. Kiln-dried wood is ok to use, but often it's actually *too* dry and it burns up quickly and produces little smoke. Bundles of small, uniform firewood logs sold at grocery stores usually are kiln-dried. You might use them in a pinch, but otherwise they're too expensive and, again, can be too dry. Never burn "green" (fresh or unseasoned) wood for cooking. It's hard to light and maintain, it smokes too much, and a lot of its heat is lost in the smoke (due to the wood's high water content). Also avoid burning moldy wood, which produces an acrid smoke.

Wood Chunks

Chunks are pieces of dried hardwood that have been split and cut into sizes from about two inches to six inches. They are commonly sold in bags at grocery and hardware stores and through barbecue supply retailers and wood suppliers. Chunks are the best all-purpose option for producing wood smoke. You can add them to a charcoal fire in a grill or smoker, and because they're nice, dry hardwood with lots of surface area, they light quickly and produce flavorful smoke in no time. This makes them ideal for dropping onto hot embers throughout the cooking process (or as long as you want to add smoke). Because chunks burn more quickly than logs, they're not economical or time-smart as a primary fuel option for large or sustained fires.

Chunks come in all the same varieties of hardwood that are popular for smoking, including oak, apple, alder, maple, cherry, mesquite, pecan, hickory, and many others. Shop around for good deals and good sources, especially local sources. You might be surprised at what's available in your area. For example, peach wood is a favorite of smokers in Georgia, for obvious reasons, but you can also find it in Colorado, where they grow peaches on the western slope of the Rockies.

Wood Chips

Wood chips are small, mulch-like pieces sold by the bag in many wood varieties. They're good for adding a bit of smoke when grilling or hot smoking. You can drop a handful onto a hot charcoal fire, repeating as needed to achieve the desired amount of smoke. Or, you can add them to a smoker box or a foil pouch and smolder the chips slowly. Chips are also used as the primary fuel for cold smoking and warm smoking in something like a smokehouse, a box-type smoker, or a small smoker like the **Clay Pot Smoker** design on page 42.

Most cooks like to soak wood chips in water before adding them to an existing fire, to make them burn more slowly. However, this is not necessary when using them as a primary fuel source. See **Should You Soak Your Wood Chips?** on page 37 for more on this subject.

Hardwood chunks add both heat and smoke to an existing fire.

Chips add lots of smoke and a small amount of heat.

Sawdust adds smoke with the least amount of heat (top). Pellets burn hotter but are easily controlled for various smoking processes (bottom).

Sawdust & Pellets

Sawdust for smoking is processed from hardwoods, typically hickory and maple. Pellets are compressed sawdust and are available in many single wood types and in blends, such as oak-hickory-cherry or oak-apple. Always use sawdust sold for smoking or cooking to be sure it doesn't contain unsavory additives or contaminants.

Sawdust is often used in smoker boxes and trays, for cold and warm smoking and for adding smoke when grilling. It should smolder, not flare up, so it doesn't make sense to add it to an existing fire. It burns (when smoldering) more slowly and creates less heat than wood chips, making it a good choice for low-heat smoking of foods like sausage and fish.

Pellets also can be used in some smoker trays and boxes, but they are primarily used in auto-feed pellet smokers. Unless you're a mechanical engineer or are a modern-day Rube Goldburg, you probably won't be building one of these yourself. Pellets burn hotter yet more slowly than wood chips, making them suitable for some hot smoking processes with the right type of smoker.

Charcoal

If you're new to grilling or at least charcoal grilling, it might surprise you to learn that charcoal is a wood product. It's produced by burning wood in a kiln at very high temperatures and with very little oxygen present. This burns off organic compounds, moisture, gasses, and other components and leaves little more than carbon. Charcoal comes in two basic forms: lump and briquettes.

Lump Charcoal

Also called *pure* or *natural* charcoal, lump charcoal is charred wood in its natural form. There's nothing added, and the pieces are randomly shaped and sized—however they come out of the burning process. Because charcoal comes from wood, it's no surprise that you can find lump charcoal in different wood species, like oak, maple, cherry, apple, and mesquite. While the source wood of charcoal can impart some flavor to the food, it's not as effective at flavoring as adding regular wood chunks or chips of the same wood.

Charcoal Briquettes

Briquettes start out as natural-wood charcoal, but then it is pulverized and combined with additives before it is shaped into the familiar rounded lumps.

A QUICK GUIDE TO WOOD TYPES

There are many ways to categorize woods for smoking: how they burn, how strong their flavor is, where they come from, what kinds of food they're traditionally used for, etc. Because most cooks are ultimately looking for flavor, perhaps the best way too group woods is by the character of their smoke.

Mild woods are characterized by sweetness and mild, if not deep, smokiness. They are popular for fish, poultry, and pork:

- Alder (mildest)
- Apple
- Cherry

Full-flavored woods are good all-arounders and are popular for most meats, seafood, and vegetables:

- Oak
- Hickory

Strong woods can be too aggressive for many foods, especially when burned without other, milder woods. They're popular for adding flavor to grilled food and for smoking red meat and game:

- Mesquite
- Walnut

WHY DOES SMOKE TASTE GOOD?

The smoke from a wood-burning fire smells undeniably good, but that doesn't make anyone want to nibble on a piece of charcoal. So what is it about smoke that has such a magical effect on food? Actually, it's not so much the smoke that we see but the gasses released with the smoke that give the food its coveted smokiness. The gasses contain aromatic wood compounds, called *phenols*, that both flavor and color the food.

Different phenols are released at different fire temperatures, and each imparts its own flavor, such as vanilla or caramel. Artisans and commercial operations may keep fires at controlled temperatures to highlight one flavor or another, but for most cooks the ideal temperature for phenols—and flavor—is about 750°F. That's the temperature of the fire, not the air inside the cooker.

Wood smoke consists of three main elements: solids (carbon particles), liquid (water, oil, tar), and gases (some containing phenols). When a fire is young and relatively cool, the solid and liquid particles are large, resulting in thick, dark smoke that leaves carbon deposits, or soot, on the food. A hot fire burns wood more completely, resulting in finer particles. The invisible wood gasses are allowed to do their thing without sooty or ashy buildup on the food. That's why it's important to maintain a proper fire that burns added fuel evenly without an excess of heavy, sooty smoke.

That shape is no accident; it ensures that air flows evenly through the briquettes even when they're piled up. The additives in briquettes vary by brand and type, but some common ingredients are coal, borax, limestone, and corn starch. Some brands also use sand, which explains the little dunes you may have seen at the bottom of your kettle grill. There are "natural" briquettes that have no additives other than a vegetable-based binder.

NOTE: Avoid charcoal briquettes with lighter fluid added so they can be started with a match. This is not the kind of fuel smoke you want on your food. Even if you start the coals away from the cooking fire, you can't be sure all of the petroleum has burned off. It's also best not to use lighter fluid when starting coals; see **Lighting a Charcoal Fire** on page 35.

Lump vs. Briquettes

Looking at sales figures alone, briquettes far outsell lump charcoal in the general marketplace, but among serious grillers and smokers, lump has many devoted fans. Here are the basic pros and cons of each:

Lump charcoal burns hotter and cleaner; you can throw fresh pieces on a fire and not worry about off-tasting smoke hitting your food. It also produces less ash, and there are no additives you have to think about. On the downside, lump burns out more quickly and burns less evenly, due to its irregular shapes and sizes.

Briquettes burn longer and more consistently, requiring less tending and replenishing. On the downside, they create more ash, and they can produce an unsavory smoke when they first ignite; for this reason, it's a good idea to start new coals separately from the grill or smoker before adding them to your cooking fire. Then there are the additives to come to terms with: Some cooks don't like the idea of coal smoke and other (often unknown) additives on their food; others feel that pre-burning new coals before adding them to the cooking fire or letting a new fire get to temperature before adding any food takes care of any concerns of toxins or bad flavors.

How to Light and Maintain a Fire

Mastering grilling and smoking is mostly about mastering the fire. This can take years of experience, experimentation, and fine-tuning of technique. It's also most of the fun of serious grilling and smoking (apart from the eating, of course). Getting a fire started is the easiest part, and maintaining it properly just takes some attention and good judgment. If you're smoking, you'll also probably spend a lot of time checking the thermometer.

Lighting a Wood Fire

Most people have a preferred method of lighting a wood fire, experience gained from scouting challenges, camping trips, or lighting fireplace fires at home. The same technique should work just fine for cooking fires, unless it involves lighter fluid or other petroleum-based fire starters, which create nasty smoke and might gunk up your cooker. You can't go wrong with plain kindling wood and some newspaper. This is particularly recommended for starting a fire in a pizza oven. Alternatively, if you're planning to use a mix of charcoal and wood, the easiest method is to start the charcoal first (see below), then add the wood.

Lighting a Charcoal Fire

There are numerous tools and methods for lighting charcoal: chimney starters, wax squares, electric starters, even blow torches. All of these are just fine. The one common method you don't want to use is lighter fluid (or instant-start charcoal with added lighter fluid). Lots of cooks use it and never have a problem, but if it's not burned off completely, you can taste it in your food. Charcoal lights easily enough without it, so it's not worth the risk.

Lump charcoal looks like charred wood.

Charcoal briquettes look like . . . charcoal briquettes.

HOW TO USE A CHIMNEY STARTER

Many cooks like chimney starters because they don't need lighter fluid and they ignite the coals evenly so when you add them to the fire there aren't any big cold spots. You can use a chimney starter for lump charcoal or charcoal briquettes:

1. Fill the bottom of the chimney starter with crumpled newspaper and fill the rest with charcoal.

2. Light the newspaper with a match. Let the coals burn until they are covered with a light layer of ash.

3. Pour the coals onto the coal grate or fire grate of your cooker. Time to cook!

Adding Wood to a Fire

There are a few tricks to learn about adding wood to either a wood fire or a charcoal fire. The first and most important is not adding too much at once. When wood ignites and starts to burn, it creates a lot of dense, white smoke. This is good for flavoring food but only in limited amounts. The better smoke comes when the wood burns hot, producing a much lighter, blue-tinged haze. This is the smoke you want for the majority of the cooking process.

It's fine to have some white smoke when you're adding new wood, but throwing too much wood on a fire and creating lots of white smoke can give the food a bitter flavor and contributes to over-smoking, resulting in a sharpness that can have a numbing effect on the tongue.

The second trick to adding wood is to do it gently, preferably using tongs or fireplace gloves. Tossing wood onto burning embers stirs up ash that can land on the food.

The final trick is the trickiest: knowing when and how much wood to add. This varies widely, depending on the cooker, the wood, the outdoor temperature, the rate of ventilation, and the food and how quickly you want it to cook and/or how much smoke it should get. As with most aspects of grilling and smoking, experience is the best teacher, but here are some general suggestions for how much wood you'll need to add:

- Wood chunks: two to four medium-size pieces every hour
- Wood chips: 1½ to 2 cups every 30–45 minutes, when adding to a fire; when smoking with chips in a pan (or grilling with a foil pouch or smoker box), replace the chips once they stop smoking, perhaps every 40–50 minutes
- Logs: one to three pieces every hour after the fire is going well

Adding Charcoal to a Fire

You can add lump charcoal directly to your cooking fire. No pre-lighting or starting is necessary. Depending on the heat of the fire and the size and type of coals, you'll likely need to add 10 or 15 pieces every hour or so. Scatter the new coals around the fire so they're not all in one place. Increase the ventilation as needed until the coals ignite, then lower it back to your cooking rate.

When adding charcoal briquettes to a fire, it's best to start the new coals separately, using a chimney starter or other method. Once the coals are covered with ash, add them to the cooking fire. Charcoal briquettes tend to give off an unsavory smoke during the initial burn, and starting them away from the cooking fire keeps this smoke away from your food. It also makes it easy to replenish your fire without a lot of monkeying with vents and opening doors to make sure the coals are starting.

SHOULD YOU SOAK YOUR WOOD CHIPS?

There are a lot of opinions for and against soaking, but the bottom line is, you *don't have to* soak them, so try it both ways and see which you prefer. Soaking is most commonly done before adding chips to a burning charcoal fire, to make the chips last a bit longer before they turn to ash. It also adds a bit of moisture to the air inside the cooker. Some people soak their chips overnight, while many chip manufacturers and expert grillers say 30 minutes is sufficient. Always drain the chips well before throwing them on the fire.

SMOKERS & OVENS

Backyard Barbecue Your Way

There is nothing quite like a well-smoked piece of meat or fish, or the crispy crust of a four-cheese pizza baked outdoors. Those are distinctive flavors and textures even among cookout foods, and they share a unique method of outdoor cooking: indirect heat.

A smoker uses a separate firebox to create heat and smoke that cooks the food slowly. An outdoor oven generally works more quickly, but the idea is the same. The heat source is kept separate from the food itself, heating the environment rather than directly cooking the food.

Outdoor ovens can be very basic because the heat source is often burned in the same space as the food. You don't even necessarily need a door. Many outdoor ovens are just large caves crafted of bricks and mortar. The do, however, require some sort of vent—usually a chimney. Regardless of the design, they aren't limited to baking pizza; an outdoor oven can also be used to bake bread or even to cook dishes such as casseroles or pies (as long as you have experience with the dish and can tell when it's done).

Crafting and cooking with a smoker is a bit more complex. Because a smoker's heat source is entirely separate from the cooking chamber, the temperatures are always relatively low. That's why it takes a good amount of time to smoke even small cuts of meat. Unfortunately, this doesn't mean you can "set and forget it." The trick to proper smoking is to maintain an even temperature by closely monitoring and feeding the firebox as needed. You also have to ensure that the smoke is flowing efficiently into the cooking chamber, and that the chamber is properly vented to alleviate pressure buildup. A wonderful side effect of the process is that the smoke impregnates the meat with a deep layer of crusty goodness that carries a hint of the wood's fruit.

Ovens are a more basic construction, and you'll find a typical pizza oven on page 74, which can be adapted to your own outdoor space and preferences. Because smokers are more complicated, there are several ways to build one. The three in this chapter represent different sizes and varying degrees of difficulty. Tackle the one you feel most comfortable executing, and that will serve your smoking needs best.

Clay Pot Smoker

A clay pot smoker is proof that you can make a smoker with pretty much anything. You may have seen smokers constructed from filing cabinets, old refrigerators, and even cardboard boxes, but a clay pot is one of the most natural adaptations. For one thing, cooking in terra cotta vessels is a traditional method in many cultures. Clay distributes and stores heat well and it holds in moisture to prevent drying out the food. A planter pot has just the right shape for a small cooker, being smaller at the bottom and larger at the top, where you want more space for food. It also looks good enough to leave out when you're not cooking (but couldn't be easier to store).

The trick to building this simple smoker is to coordinate the shopping so all the main parts fit together. This includes a large pot for the cooking vessel, a shallow pot for the lid, a round grill grate, and an electric hot plate. When choosing the parts, make sure:

- The hot plate fits on the flat bottom of the cooking pot.
- The grill grate fits inside the top of the cooking pot, and preferably rests on a ridge near the top of the pot.
- The pot for the lid fits onto the rim of the cooking pot (when the lid is upside down) and has a flat bottom for the handle assembly.

This smoker is suitable for smoking at temperatures up to about 225°F. (see **Smoking Temperatures: Cold, Warm, and Hot** on page 25). Use wood chips in a metal pie plate or pan on top of the electric hot plate for hot smoking. For smoking at lower temperatures, you can leave the hot plate off (or remove it from the pot) and smoke with sawdust inside a cold smoker tray (see **Cold Smokers** on page 28). Check the thermometer frequently when smoking because the temperature can fluctuate easily in such as small unit.

TOOLS & MATERIALS

- Drill-driver
- 1¼" carbide hole saw (for ceramic tile)
- ¼" wood drill bit
- ¼" and ½" tile or masonry drill bits
- Scissors
- Adjustable wrenches
- Eye and ear protection
- Work gloves
- 16" or larger deep clay pot (for the cooking pot) (1)
- 16" or larger water saucer (for lid) (1)
- Electric hot plate (1,000 – 1,200 watts) (1)
- ½"-wide heatproof self-adhesive gasket tape; 5 linear feet min.
- 1¼"-diameter × 5"–6"-long hardwood dowel (1)
- ¼ × 4½" stainless-steel flathead stove bolts (2) with washers and nuts (6)
- Barbecue thermometer with mounting nut (1)
- Wine corks (natural cork) (2)
- 60-grit sandpaper
- Clay pot feet (3 or 4)
- 8"-diameter heavy aluminum pie plate (1)

How to Build the Clay Pot Smoker

TIP

Drill a 1¼"-diameter (or as needed) hole through the bottom of the cooking pot, using a drill and a carbide hole saw (for ceramic tile). This hole must be big enough for the hot plate cord plug to fit through. Drill the hole in any convenient location, but stay a few inches away from any preexisting drain holes in the pot.

Apply heatproof gasket tape along the top edge of the cooking pot. Trim excess at the end with scissors.

NOTE: The gasket tape creates a seal between the cooking pot and the lid. If this joint leaks smoke when you're using the smoker, add a layer of gasket tape to the edge of the lid.

Create the lid handle with a 5" to 6" length of hardwood dowel. Drill two ¼" holes through the dowel for support bolts, spacing the holes so the bolts will be inside the flat area on the bottom of the lid. Insert two ¼ × 4½" stove bolts through the handle, and secure each with a washer and nut. Tighten the nuts and washer against the underside of the handle.

Install the handle by drilling ¼" holes for the handle bolts through the bottom of the lid pot, using a ¼" tile or masonry bit. Secure the handle to the lid with a washer and nut on both the top and the underside of the lid. Tighten the nuts toward each other, being careful not to overtighten them and crack the lid.

Install the thermometer by drilling a ¼" hole in a convenient location on the lid. Insert the thermometer probe end into the hole and secure it on the inside of the lid with the provided nut.

Drill two ½" ventilation holes near the top of the lid, on opposite sides of the handle, using a ½" tile or masonry bit. Use coarse sandpaper to shave down a wine cork to fit snugly into each hole. Your smoker is ready to use; see **Setting Up Your Clay Pot Smoker** (below).

SETTING UP YOUR CLAY POT SMOKER

Place the cooking pot onto three or four pot feet (also called pot toes) on a stable, noncombustible surface. Set the hot plate unit into the bottom of the pot, feeding the cord through the 1½" hole in the bottom. Plug the hot plate into a grounded electrical outlet. If the pot will be exposed to the elements, make sure the outlet is GFCI-protected to protect against a shock hazard. If you need to use an extension cord, make sure the cord is rated for at least fifteen amps. Hot plates can draw a lot of power, which can overheat an undersized cord.

Fill a pie plate with a layer of wood chips, about one inch deep. As you use your smoker, you will fine-tune the amount of chips to use as well as the temperature setting of the hot plate. Plug in the hot plate and turn it on. With a 1,000-watt hot plate, a medium-low to medium heat setting will probably create a warm-smoking temperature of about 165°F, but this may vary widely. Place the pie plate onto the hot plate burner.

Set the grill grate into the cooking pot, and place your food onto the grate. Cover the pot with the lid, and you're smoking! Check the thermometer frequently until it levels off within the desired temperature range. Also check the wood chips every 45 minutes to 1 hour; when the chips are completely burned to ash, dump the ash into a pan of water or a noncombustible container, and refill the pan with chips.

Plug the ventilation holes to increase the smoke intensity, as desired.

Smokehouse

A smokehouse is a special kind of smoker. While most other smokers are essentially modified barbecue grills, a smokehouse is an entire building devoted to smoking. It has a full-size door (or in this case, two doors) and lots of roomy shelves that are in full view when the door is open. It even has a hook for hanging large cuts of meat.

As a hand-built wood structure, a smokehouse also looks nothing like other smokers. And as good as it looks just standing out back, imagine how much better it looks with fragrant smoke pouring out of it like a steam engine. (Although you might want to let your neighbors know about it so they aren't alarmed when they see your new "shed" smoldering, and you probably should share some of the food with them so they aren't so jealous they call the fire department anyway.)

A smokehouse is designed for cold and warm smoking only, using wood chips, pellets, or sawdust (see **Smoking Temperatures: Cold, Warm, and Hot** on page 25). It has fire-resistant materials at its base, and this is where you can set up a smoker tray (see **Cold Smokers** on page 28) or an electric burner with a pan full of wood chips. In all cases, the "fire" simply smolders, and it must be contained within a fireproof vessel, such as a cold smoker or pan. The smokehouse is not suitable for any kind of open fire with flames or for burning embers.

The double-door of this smokehouse design provides easy access to the base area for replenishing fuel without having to open up the main door and let out all the heat. Another special design feature is the panelized construction: the walls are made with plywood siding, and you build all four walls, including the trim and interior elements, on a flat surface. When the walls are done, you tip them up and screw them together, then add the roof and doors.

The smokehouse shown here was made with cedar plywood siding and cedar lumber trim. Cedar is a good option because it's lightweight and easy to work worth, and it looks great on a small structure like this with a lot of trim. It also has some natural resistance to decay and weathering, although this varies considerably with different grades of lumber. As with all other woods, cedar needs a UV-resistant exterior finish (on the outside only; do not finish the smokehouse interior) if you don't want it to turn gray with weathering. The masonry base, which serves as the smokehouse floor, can be a stone or precast concrete slab or simply patio pavers.

NOTE: Many of the project dimensions are based on the actual dimensions (thickness and/or width) of the siding and trim material. Measure your materials carefully and adjust the given dimensions as needed.

SMOKEHOUSE

TOOLS & MATERIALS

- Circular saw
- Power miter saw (optional)
- Jigsaw
- Hammer
- 2' or 4' level
- Wood chisel
- Framing square
- Drill-driver
- Drill bits
- Countersink bit
- Utility knife
- Mason's blade
- Straightedge
- Caulk gun
- Tin snips
- Tape measure
- Pencil
- Eye and ear protection
- Work gloves
- 2 × 4 × 8' pressure-treated lumber (3)
- ⅝" × 4' × 8' cedar plywood siding (4)
- 2 × 2 × 8' cedar or pine lumber (6)
- 1 × 3 × 8' cedar lumber (10)
- 1 × 2 × 8' cedar lumber (14)
- 1 × 4 × 8' cedar lumber (3)
- 2 × 4 × 4' cedar or pine lumber (1)
- ½" × 3' × 5' cementboard (2)
- 1" roofing screws (30)
- 1¾" deck screws (84)
- 1" hot-dipped galvanized roofing nails (24)
- 1¼" drywall or wood screws (250)
- 2" deck screws (4)
- 16d hot-dipped galvanized common nails (16)
- 2 × 36 × 36" stone slab or concrete utility pad (1)
- Exterior (waterproof) wood glue
- Construction adhesive (for masonry and wood)
- 4"-diameter stainless-steel butterfly vents (1)
- 1"-thick scrap lumber
- 26" × 10' galvanized metal corrugated roofing (1)
- Decorative exterior door/gate hinges w/screws (5)
- Galvanized door hasps (2)
- 5/16 × 5" stainless-steel screw hook (2)
- Chrome metal wire shelving, 12" or 18" wide × 36" long; quantity as desired
- Compactible gravel or concrete pavers
- Pre-cast pavers (cut to size)
- Heatproof caulk

CUTTING LIST

KEY	PART	DIMENSIONS	PCS.	MATERIAL
A	Base joist	1½ × 3½ × 33½"	4	2 × 4 Pressure-treated pine
B	Base end joist	1½ × 3½ × 36½"	2	2 × 4 Pressure-treated pine
C	Side wall panel	⅝ × 36½ × 75"	2	⅝" Cedar plywood siding
D	Front/Rear wall panel	⅝ × 37¾ × 82"	2	⅝" Cedar plywood siding
E	Shelf support (side walls)	1½ × ½ × 36½"	8	2 × 2 Cedar or pine
F	Shelf support (rear wall)	1½ × 1½ × 33¼"	4	2 × 2 Cedar or pine
G	Cementboard (side walls)	½ × 18 × 36½"	2	½" Cementboard
H	Cementboard (rear wall)	½ × 18 × 35½"	1	½" Cementboard
I	Cementboard (lower door)	½" × Cut to fit	1	½" Cementboard
J	Corner trim (side walls)	¾ × 2½ × 74 11/16"	4	1 × 3 Cedar
K	Corner trim (front/rear wall)	¾ × 2½" × Cut to fit	4	1 × 3 Cedar
L	Base sheathing			
M	Roof ridge boards			
N	Rafters	¾ × 3½ × 28¼"	6	1 × 4 Cedar
O	Beam	1½ × 3½ × 36½"	1	2 × 4 Cedar or pine
P	Front wall bottom trim	¾ × 3½" × Cut to fit	1	1 × 4 Cedar
Q	Door header trim	¾ × 1½" × Cut to fit	1	1 × 2 Cedar
R	Roof decking	⅝ × 37¾" × Cut to fit	4	⅝" Cedar plywood siding
S	Roofing	26" × Cut to fit	4	Galvanized corrugated roofing
T	Door trim	¾ × 2½" × Cut to fit	11	1 × 3 Cedar

BASE

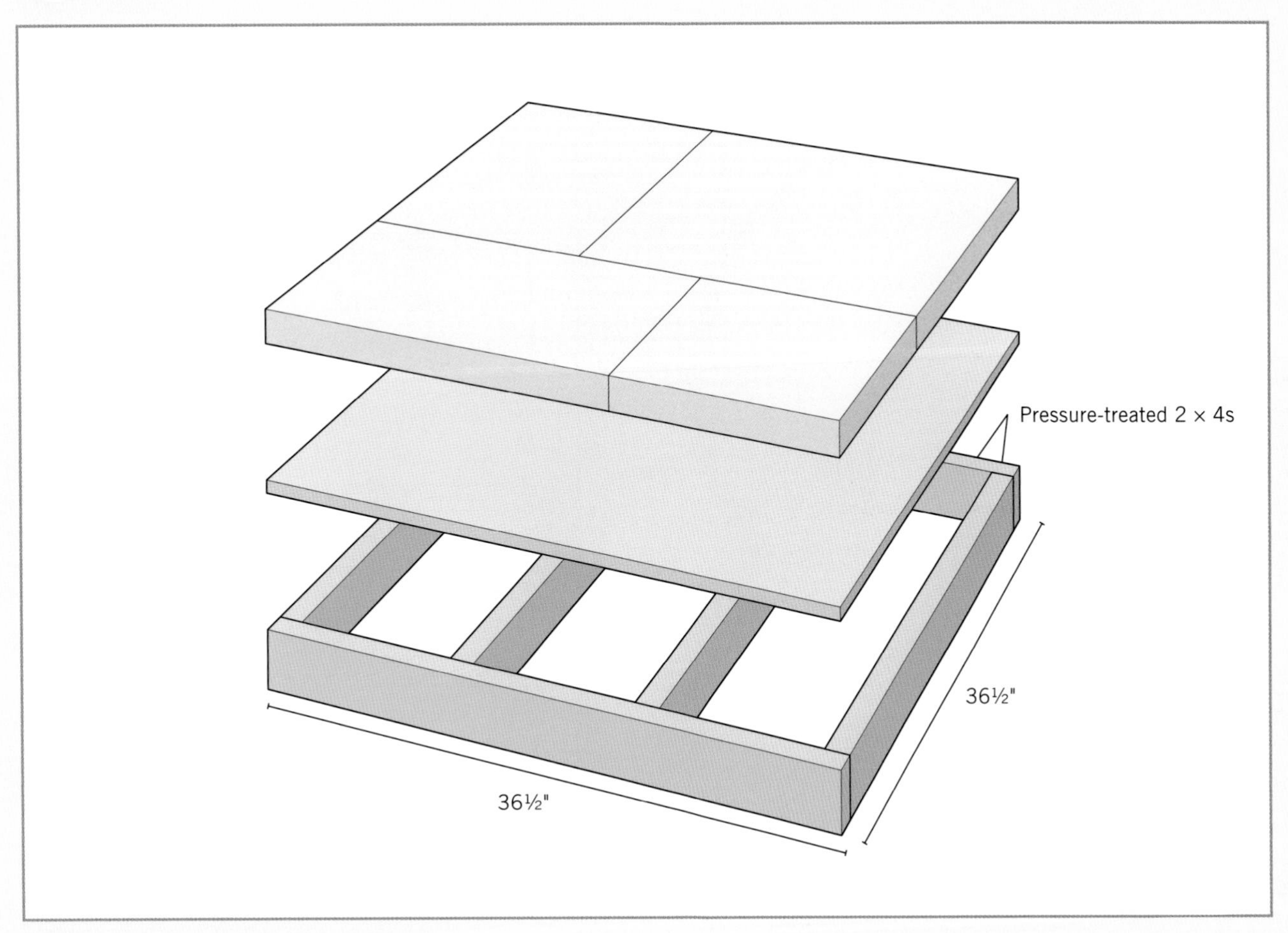

MIDDLE RAFTER & BEAM

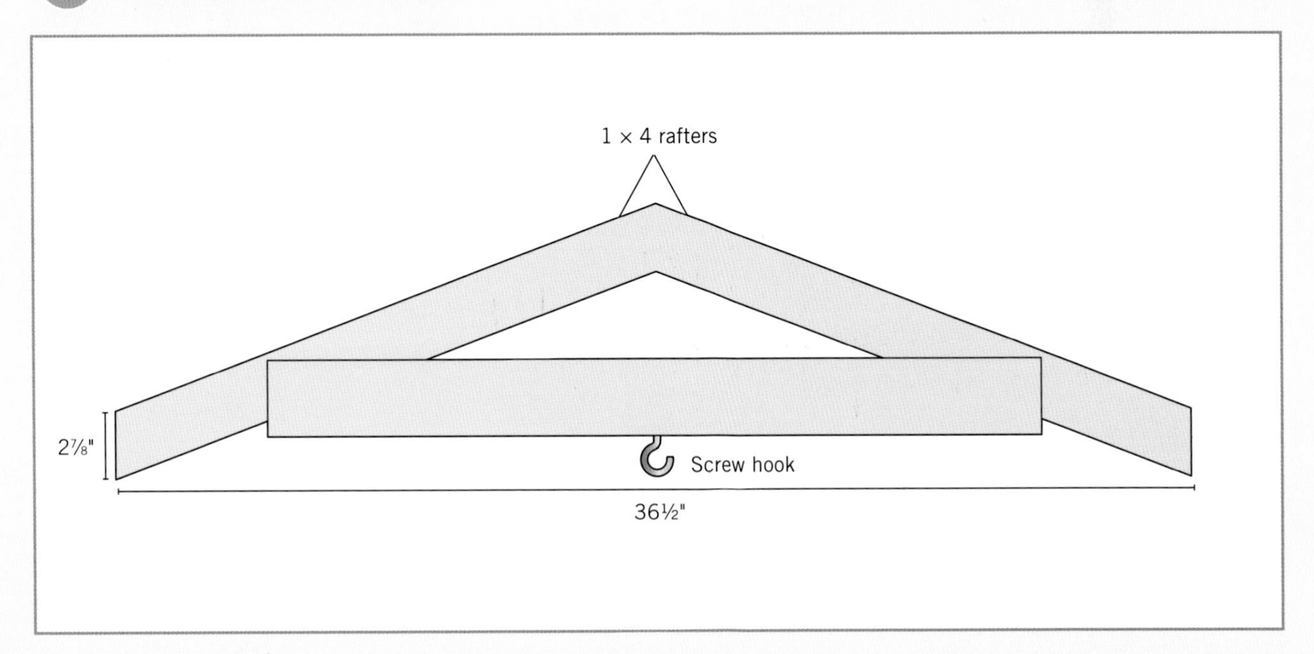

FRONT ELEVATION

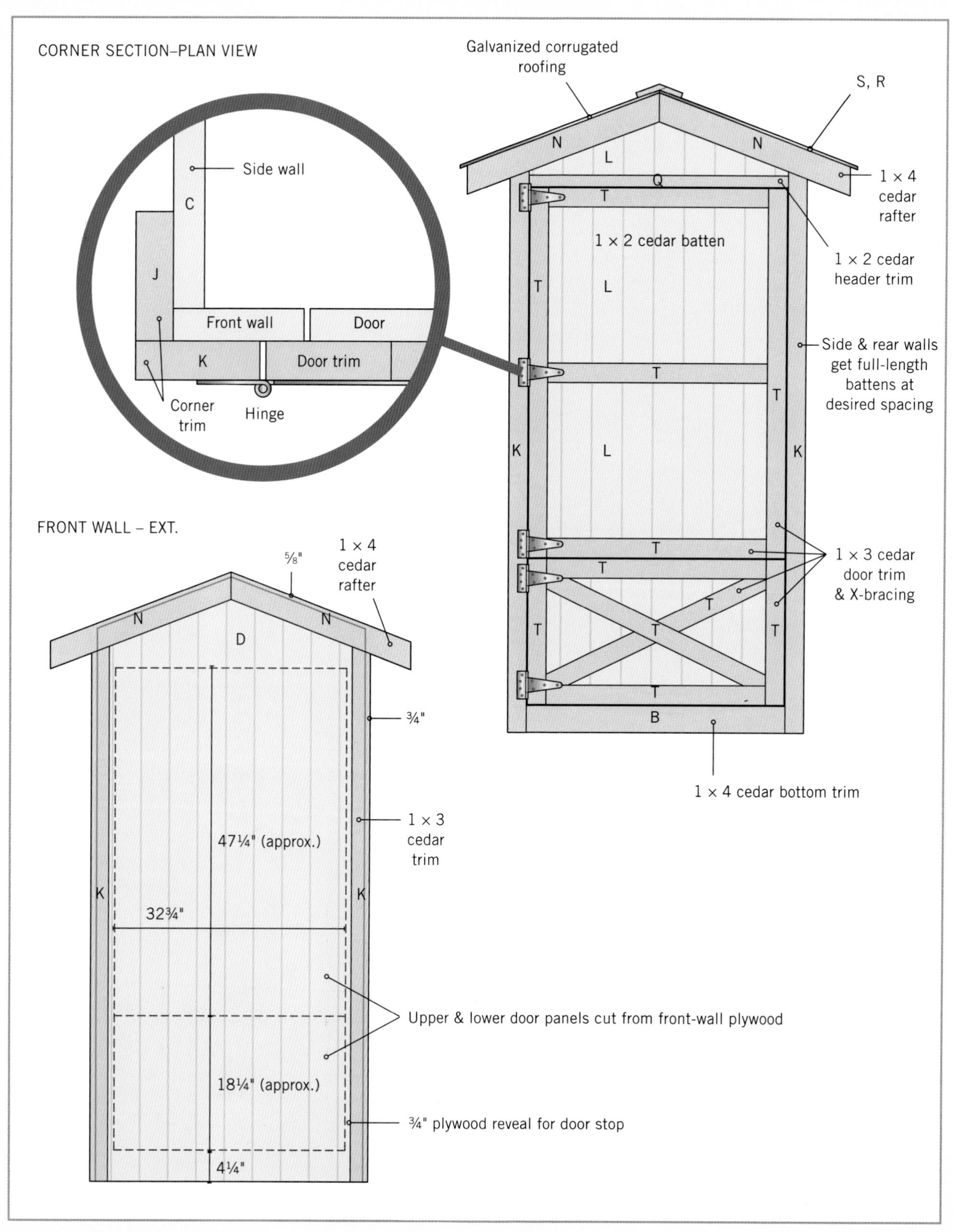

LEFT & RIGHT SIDE WALLS—INTERIOR

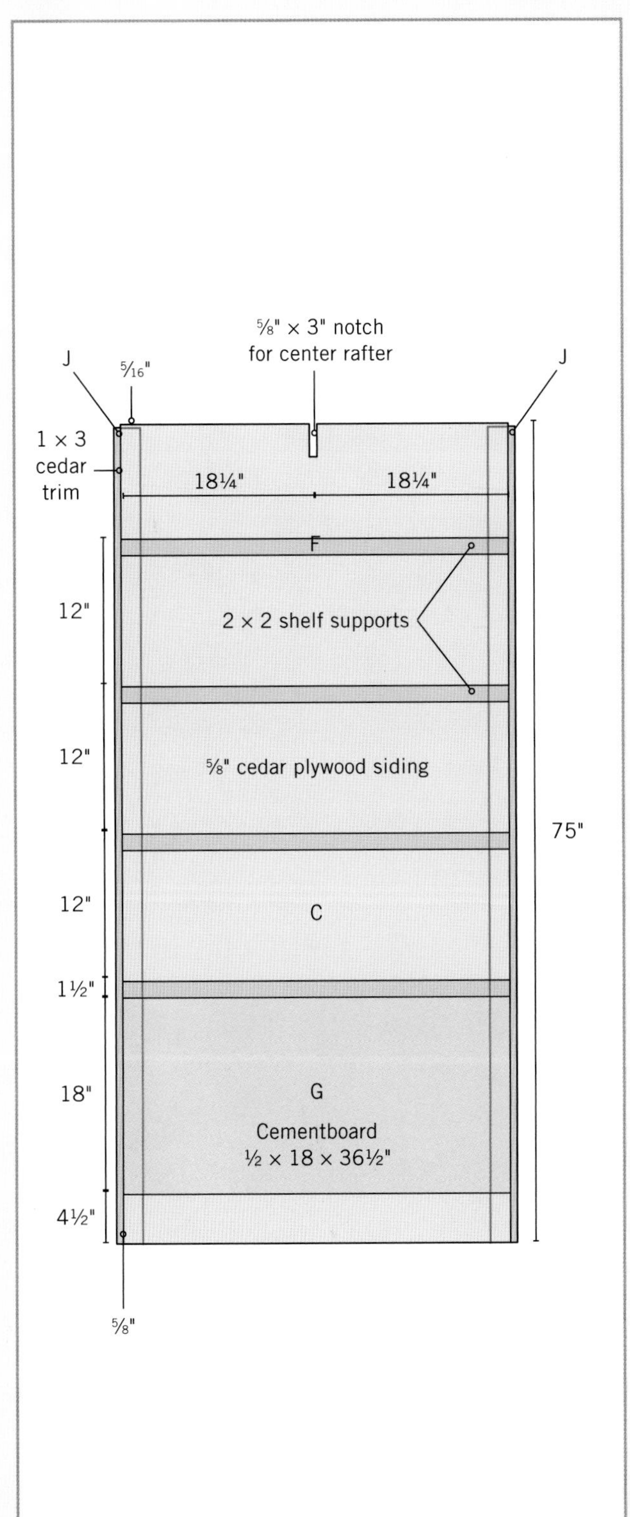

REAR WALL—INTERIOR

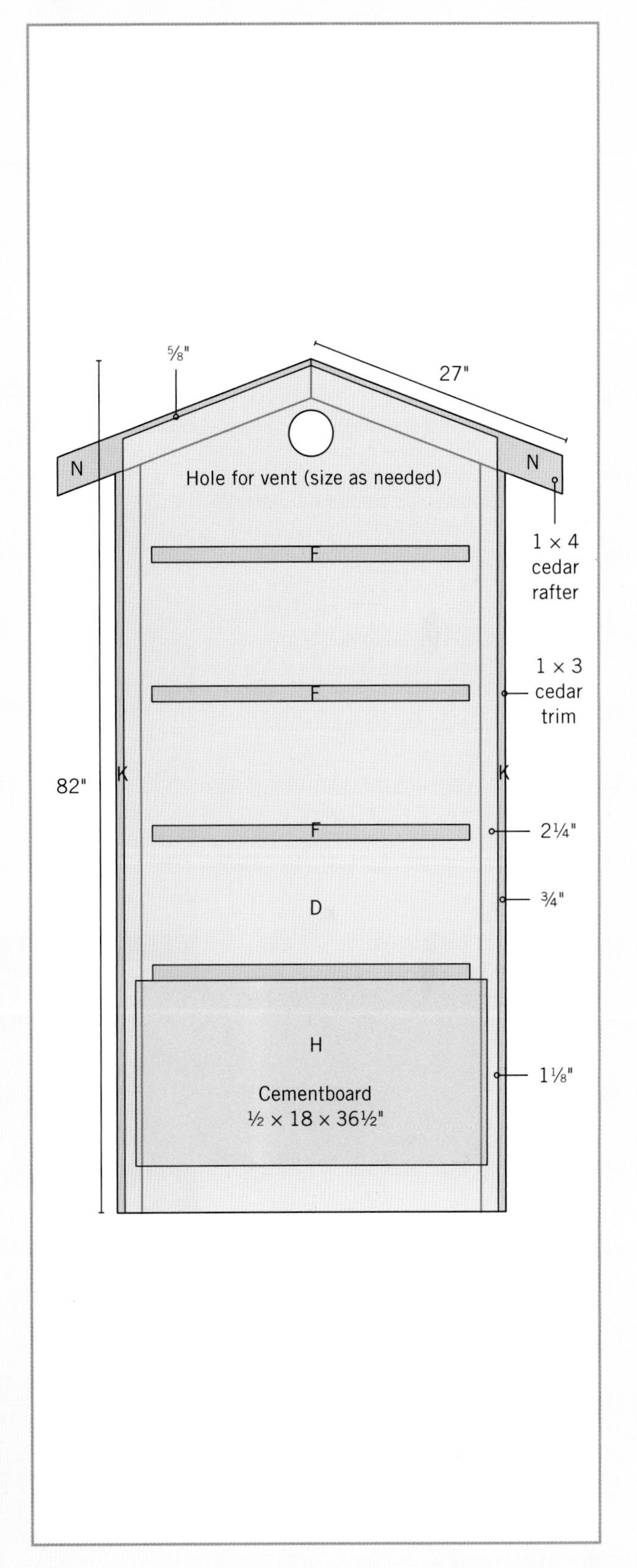

How to Build the Smokehouse

Build the base frame by cutting the base joist and end joist pieces to length from pressure-treated 2 × 4s. Set the pieces on-edge and assemble the base by fitting the end joists over the ends of the base joists. Space the two center base joists evenly. Drive two 16d nails through the end joists and into each end of the base joists. Make sure all joists are flush at the top.

Set the base frame on a flat, level, stable surface, preferably an area that drains well. Good options include a concrete or brick patio, compacted gravel, or masonry pavers. Use a 2' or 4' level to make sure the frame is level side to side and front to back.

Cut a plywood base cover the same dimensions as the base frame and attach it to the frame with deck screws.

Install a layer of precast concrete pavers on top of the wood base. If you need to cut the pavers to fit, use a circular saw with a masonry blade to score deep lines and then break off the extra with a rubber mallet. You could also nail 2 × 4 forms around the perimeter of the base and pour a solid concrete base that's at least 1½" thick (remove the forms after one day).

Cut one of the side wall panels to size from ⅝" plywood siding. Mark the rafter notch at the center of the top edge of the panel. The notch width should be a snug fit for the rafter material you will use. Cut the sides of the notch with a circular saw or jigsaw, then cut the base of the notch with a wood chisel and/or the jigsaw.

NOTE: Save all of the leftover siding pieces for the roof deck.

Lay out the shelf support locations on the inside face of the side wall panel. The bottom shelf support should be about 18" from the top of the smokehouse base, or 22½" from the bottom edge of the side wall. The remaining shelves can be spaced as desired. Here they are spaced 12" apart. Draw lines for the top edges of the shelf supports, using a framing square.

TIP: Use this side panel as a template for marking and laying out the other side wall panel.

Cut the 2 × 2 shelf supports to length for both side walls and the rear wall. Install the shelf supports on the side wall using wood glue and 1¾" deck screws or wood screws. Cut and notch the second side wall panel, and install its shelf supports.

NOTE: For all screws in this project, drill pilot holes and countersink the holes slightly so the screw heads are flush with the wood surface. *(continued)*

Install the side wall corner trim. Cut two pieces of 1 × 3 trim for each side panel; these are 5/16 inches shorter than the panels. Install the side trim with glue and 1¼ inches drywall or wood screws. The trim should overhang the side edges by 5/8" (the thickness of the plywood siding) and be flush with the bottom edges of the panels.

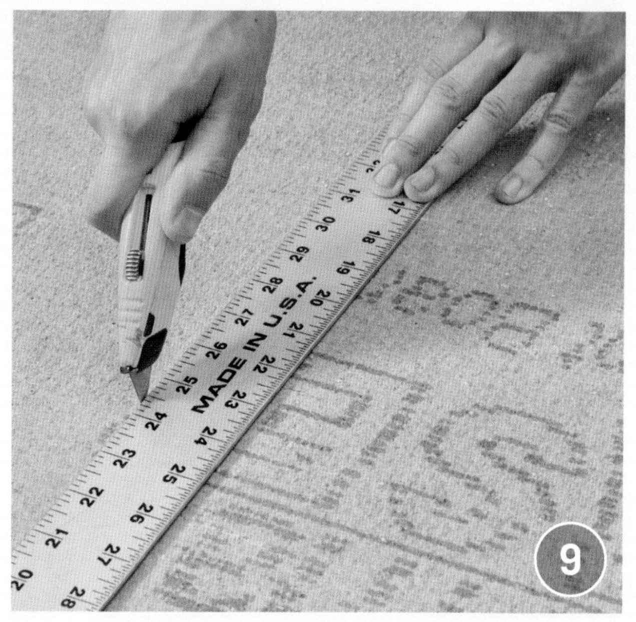

Cut a piece of cement board for each side wall using a utility knife and a straightedge. Make two or three passes with the knife to score the cutting line deeply. Snap the board backward to break it along the cutting line, then cut through the fiberglass mesh on the back side of the board.

Apply construction adhesive in wavy beads to the inside face of each side panel, then add the cementboard. Tack the board in place with several 1" roofing nails. The cementboard fits against the first shelf support. It should be flush with the side edges of the plywood and 4½" from the bottom edge of the side wall.

Prepare the rear and front wall panels. Staring with the rear wall, mark the cutting lines for the overall width and length, then mark the center of the top edge. Mark each side edge at 75" from the bottom, then draw an angled line between the side marks and the top center mark to create the roof angle. Cut the rear panel to size. Using the rear wall as a template, mark and cut the front wall to size. You will cut the door panels from the front wall later.

Cut two rafter pieces from 1 × 4 cedar lumber. Test-fit the pieces on the rear wall or they should meet at the peak of the wall and run parallel to the top wall edges. Adjust the rafter end cuts, if necessary, for a good fit. Using one of the rafters as a template, mark and cut the remaining four rafter pieces. Install a pair of rafters on the outside face of the rear wall, using glue and 1¼" screws, as with the side-wall trim. The rafters should be ⅝" above the top edges of the rear wall: this creates a recess for the roof decking. Add the corner trim and battens (as desired) to the rear wall.

Install the shelf supports and cementboard on the inside face of the rear wall, following the same techniques used for the side walls. The shelf supports should be 2¼" from each side edge of the plywood panel. The cementboard should be 1⅛" from the side edges and 4½" from the bottom edge of the plywood.

Make the hole for the vent following the vent manufacturer's specifications. Use the vent itself to mark the hole, or use a compass. Drill a ¼" starter hole just inside the cutting line for inserting the jigsaw blade, then cut out the circle with a jigsaw. The vent (when installed) should be close as practical to the rafters and centered side to side on the rear wall.

(continued)

Mark the cutting lines for the door opening onto the interior face of the front wall panel. The upper and lower door panels will come from the piece cut out for the opening. Make the initial cuts with a circular saw, then use a jigsaw to complete the cuts at the corners. Remove the cutout piece, then make the horizontal cut to create the two door panels. You can adjust the relative lengths of the two doors; just make sure the lower door is tall enough to allow easy access to your smoker tray or burner.

Complete the front wall panel by installing the rafters and corner trim, as with the rear wall. Install the 1 × 2 header trim so it butts against the corner trim and is set ¾" above the top edge of the door opening. This ¾" reveal will serve as a doorstop. Add the battens above the header trim. Install the 1 × 4 bottom trim flush with the bottom edge of the wall panel to create a ¾" reveal.

Make the hole for the vent on the front wall panel, as with the rear wall. Install the vents on the front and rear walls, following the manufacturer's instructions.

Construct the middle rafter assembly by trimming ⅝" from the top edge of each of the remaining two rafters. Cut the 2 × 4 beam to length. Join the rafters together at the peak with glue, then drive a 2" deck screw at an angle through the top of one rafter and into the end of the other. Reinforce the joint where the rafters meet with a plywood gusset secured with 1" screws. Fasten the rafters to the beam with glue and 2" screws driven through the rafters and into the beam. The rafters should extend past the beam equally on both sides.

Prepare for the wall assembly by placing 1"-thick spacers (of scrap wood or other material) along all four sides of the smokehouse base. With a helper, set the rear wall and one of the side walls onto the spacers, and join the walls by driving 2" deck screws through the corner trim of the rear wall and into the trim of the side wall. Also screw through the outside of each wall and into the base with a pair of screws every 6". Repeat with the other side wall, then the front wall.

Fit the middle rafter assembly into the notches of the side walls. The tops of the rafters should be flush with the outside corners of the side-wall plywood. Cut two pieces of roof decking (from leftover siding) to size at 21 × 37¾". Position each piece at the lower side of the roof, flush with the ends of the rafters, and fasten it to the middle rafter and front and rear wall panels with 1¾" deck screws. Cut and install two more plywood pieces to complete the roof deck on each side. *(continued)*

Cut a full-width piece of metal roofing to length for each side of the roof, using tin snips. You can also use a circular saw or jigsaw with a metal-cutting blade. Install the roofing with 1" roofing screws. Cut and install a second piece for each side, overlapping the first piece by at least one corrugation.

Finish the roof peak with two strips of leftover plywood or trim material. Cut a 40° bevel along one long edge of each piece so the pieces fit together at the roof peak, with one piece overlapping the other.

Measure the width of the door opening and subtract ¼"; use this dimension for overall width of the doors. Cut door panels to size. Install the 1 × 3 door trim along the sides and top of the upper door panel, using glue and 1¼" screws, as with the corner trim on the walls. The side trim overhangs the door panel as needed to match the overall width dimension. Overhang the top of the door a similar amount, and position the bottom trim flush with the bottom of the door panel. Place the center horizontal trim at door's center. Hang the door with exterior hinges, maintaining a ¼" gap at the side and top edges.

OPTION: Finish the exterior of the smokehouse, if desired. An exterior stain or other penetrating finish is recommended. The wide temperature and humidity changes inside the smoke may cause problems for paint. Do not finish the smokehouse interior.

Add trim to the lower door panel, as with the upper door. The top horizontal trim should be flush with the top edge of the door panel. To cut the X-brace trim, lay a full piece of 1 × 3 diagonally from the upper left corner to the lower right corner, and mark where it intersects the side and top trim. Cut the piece and fit it into place, then do the same with two pieces angled in the opposite direction. Cut and install a piece of cementboard to cover the inside of the door. Hang the door with two hinges.

Drill a pilot hole for the screw hook into the bottom edge of the 2 × 4 beam. Drive in the hook initially by hand, then use large pliers or a tool handle for leverage. Drive until all of the threads are buried in the wood. Add metal wire shelving onto the shelf supports. If necessary, cut the shelves to length with the jigsaw and a metal-cutting blade.

Fill the gaps between pavers with heatproof caulk to prevent cinders from migrating onto the plywood base.

Double-Barrel Smoker

The double-barrel grill is considered by many to be the true barbecue smoker. It has two separate chambers: a *firebox* for the fire and a *smoke chamber* for the food. The smoke and some of the heat from the fire flow into the smoke chamber and circulate around the food on their way to the chimney at one end of the smoke chamber. This design is ideal for providing lots of smoke while maintaining a target temperature between 225° and 275°F. that's desired for most barbecue meats.

Most commercial double-barrel grills (also known as *offset smokers*) have a small barrel-shaped firebox located at one end of the smoke chamber, but this style is difficult to build without a lot of welding, including fabricating your own firebox. The stacked-barrel design shown here is easier to build because it simply uses two complete steel drums, and no welding is required. The design follows the basic configuration of a traditional double-barrel woodstove, and it uses a woodstove kit that includes an iron door for the firebox and a flue assembly that creates the channel between the two barrels.

This type of woodstove kit is widely available from woodstove and fireplace suppliers and many online retailers. Kits often include metal feet for the barrels, but these are not used in the smoker project as shown. The bottoms of the barrels are lined with firebrick to help retain heat and maintain even temperatures throughout the cooking process.

When sourcing drums for your project, look for *unlined*, plain steel (not galvanized) drums that are new (preferably) or have not contained any toxic materials. Drums that are not unlined may contain a plastic coating on the interior that may emit toxic fumes when the drum is heated. The drums shown here are standard 30-gallon barrels, which measure about 18 inches diameter and 27 inches long and yield about 480 square inches of cooking surface in the smoke chamber. You can also use 55-gallon drums with the same type of woodstove kit, if you prefer a larger cooker.

Be sure to use *tight head* or *closed head* drums; these have permanently attached (nonremovable) heads.

WARNING: Remove all bungs (threaded plugs in the drum heads) before drilling, cutting, or grinding any part of a drum. If the bungs are not removed, heated air trapped inside the drum can cause the drum to explode.

DOUBLE-BARREL SMOKER

TOOLS & MATERIALS

30-gallon unlined steel barrels (2)
Barrel stove kit (with door and flue parts)
Duct tape
1 × 1 × 96" aluminum square tubing (2)
1 × 1 × 48" aluminum square tubing (1)
1 × 1 × 96" aluminum angle (1)
¼ × 2½" stainless-steel hex bolts with washers and nuts (14)
¼ × 1½" stainless-steel bolts with washers and nuts (6)
¼ × 1" stainless-steel bolts with washers and nuts (12)
¼ × 4½" stainless-steel bolts with washers and nuts (2)
Set of 4" wheels with solid-metal axle, washers, and cap nuts
1½ × 48" 26-gauge aluminum strips (2)
⅛ × ¼" stainless-steel pop rivets (22)
⅜" sheetmetal screws (4)
½" self-drilling sheet metal screws (2)
¼ × ¾" stainless-steel bolts with washers and nuts (6)
High-temperature silicone caulk (rated for 600°F or above)
⅜ × 84" woodstove door gasket rope
Woodstove door gasket sealant
3" stainless-steel hinges (2)
17"-wide grill grate (1 or 2)
4" galvanized round metal duct elbow
4 × 24" galvanized round metal duct with damper
4" standard flue collar with crimp
4" flue pipe, 8" long (will be cut to size)
1¼"-diameter × 18" hardwood dowel
18 × 24" aluminum or galvanized expanded metal sheet
9 × 4½ × 2½" medium-duty firebricks (15)
High-temperature stove paint rated for 1,200°F. (optional)
Duct tape
Marker
Drill-driver
⅛", ¼", and ½" drill bits
Jigsaw and metal-cutting blades
Bar clamps
Strap clamps
Ratchet wrench
Small level
Scrap lumber
Metal snips
Caulk gun
Grinder and abrasive disc
Pop rivet tool
Brickset chisel
Maul
Eye and ear protection
Work gloves

NOTE: For a door kit for a barrel stove, see www.amazon.com/Vogelzang-BK100E-Barrel-Stove-Kit/dp/B0018JBFS8

CUTTING LIST

KEY	PART	DIMENSIONS	PCS.	MATERIAL
A	Frame uprights—right side	1 × 1 × 42"	2	1" square aluminum tubing
B	Frame uprights—left side	1 × 1 × 41"	2	1" square aluminum tubing
C	Frame cross pieces	1 × 1 × Cut to fit	4	1" square aluminum tubing
D	Frame angles	1 × 1 × 40½"	2	1 × 1" aluminum angle
E	Shelf	Cut to fit	1	Expanded metal sheet
F	Handle	1¼ × 17"	1	1¼" hardwood dowel

SIDE VIEW

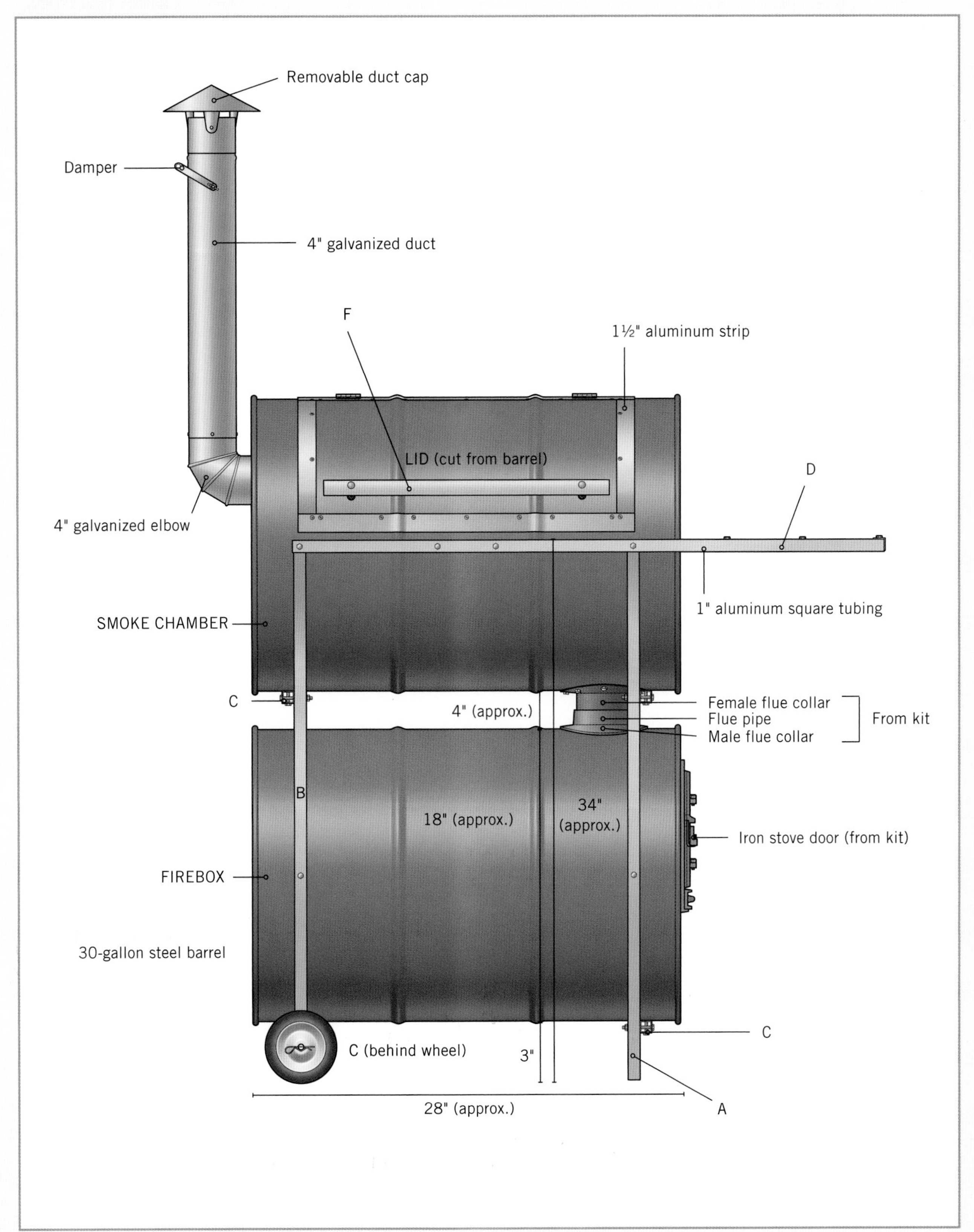

Removable duct cap
Damper
4" galvanized duct
F
1½" aluminum strip
LID (cut from barrel)
D
4" galvanized elbow
1" aluminum square tubing
SMOKE CHAMBER
C
4" (approx.)
Female flue collar
Flue pipe
Male flue collar
From kit
B
18" (approx.)
34" (approx.)
Iron stove door (from kit)
FIREBOX
30-gallon steel barrel
C
C (behind wheel)
3"
28" (approx.)
A

FIREBOX–END VIEW EXTERIOR

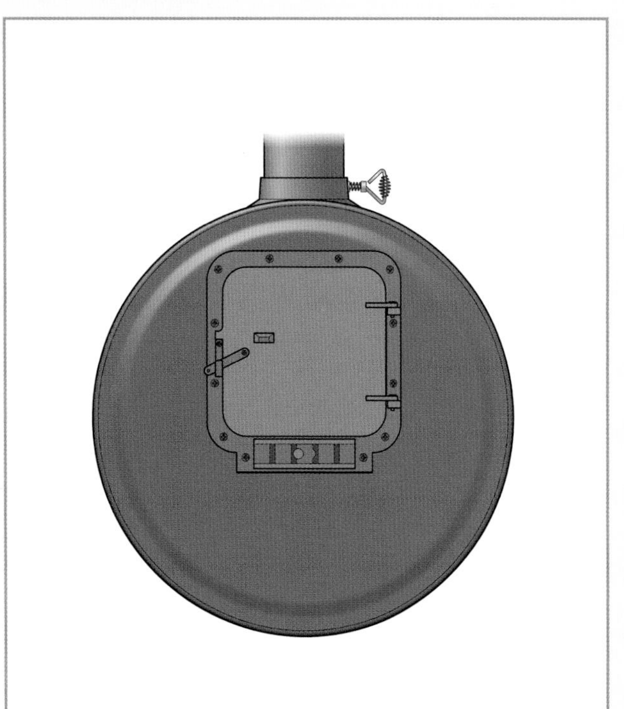

FIREBOX–END VIEW CROSS-SECTION

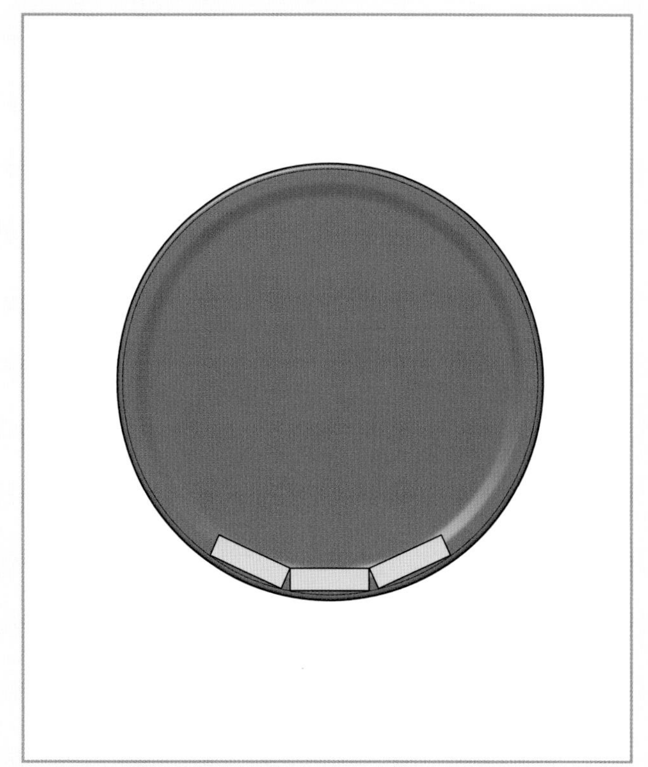

SMOKE CHAMBER–END VIEW CROSS-SECTION

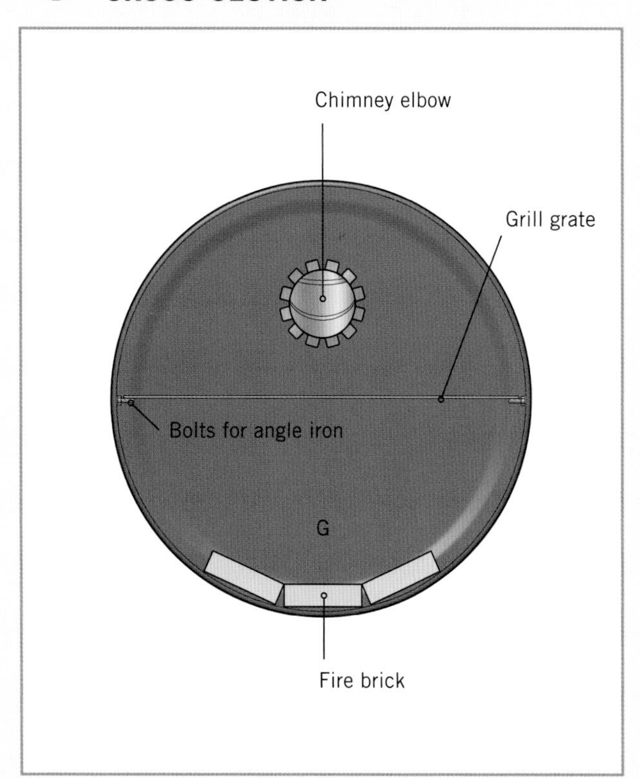

SMOKE CHAMBER–SIDE VIEW CROSS-SECTION

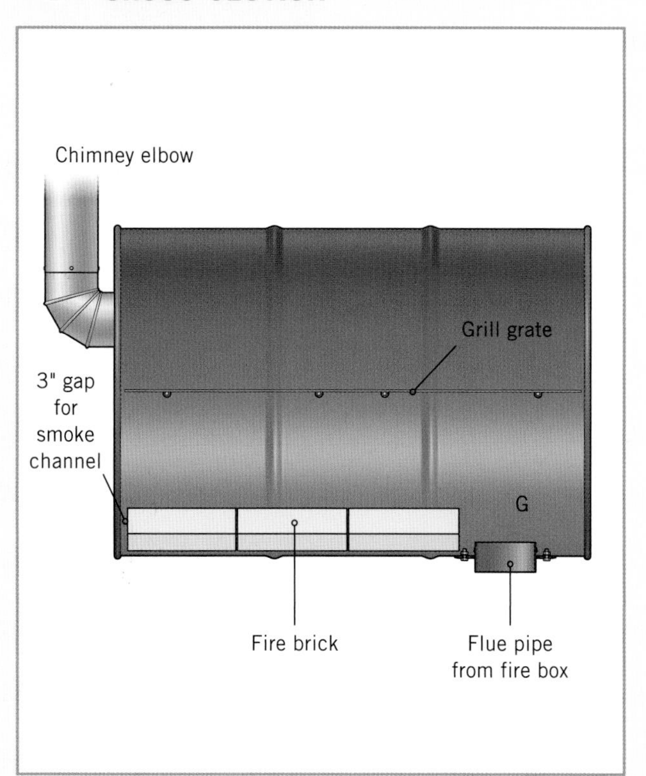

How to Build the Double-Barrel Smoker

Position the woodstove door from the stove kit over the end of the lower barrel so it is centered side to side and as close as possible to the top of the barrel. Mark the mounting bolt holes onto the barrel with a marker.

Open the door and trace onto the barrel along the inside of the door opening, as well as the vent opening, if there is a separate vent area. Remove the door and enlarge the outline as directed by the manufacturer—this is to accommodate the flange around the opening.

WARNING: Remove all plugs covering the bung holes of the barrel to prevent a buildup of pressure when drilling or cutting the barrel in the next step.

Drill a ½" starter hole inside the corners of the door opening outline. Cut out the opening with a jigsaw and metal-cutting blade, using the starter hole to initiate the cut. Drill the holes for the door mounting bolts with a ¼" bit. Cover the edges of the door opening with duct tape to protect yourself from the sharp edges.

(continued)

Support the barrel on both sides so the door opening is level. Mark a reference line on the top of the barrel to indicate the exact top of the barrel. Position the flue collar (from the stove kit) at the top center of the barrel, near an end where there is a smooth surface without ribs. Mark the collar's mounting bolt holes onto the top of the barrel, then remove the collar.

Remove the damper from the collar, then trace inside the collar onto the surface of the barrel. Drill a ½" starter hole and cut out the flue opening with a jigsaw, then drill the ¼" mounting bolt holes. Now, measure, mark, and cut a flue hole on the upper barrel to exactly align with the collar on the lower barrel. Also drill mounting bolt holes for the collar on the upper barrel.

Cut the barrel frame uprights, cross pieces, and angles to length, using a jigsaw, and adjusting the dimensions as needed to fit your barrels. The cross pieces are equal to the barrel diameter plus 2".

Begin assembling the barrel frame using the barrels to set the proper distance between the uprights. The barrels should fit snugly inside the completed frame. Clamp the cross pieces to the uprights, then drill a ¼" hole through both pieces of tubing at each joint. Secure each joint with a ¼ × 2½" threaded bolt with a washer and nut.

Install the wheels by drilling a hole through each left upright and inserting an axle through the holes. Position the holes so the barrel frame will be level when the wheels are installed. Fit the wheels onto the axle ends, using washers as applicable, and secure each wheel with a cotter pin, cap nut, or other appropriate hardware.

Mount the flue collar to the upper barrel using 1½" threaded bolts with washers and nuts. The nuts go in the inside of the barrel, so you will have to reach through the flue opening to install them.

(continued)

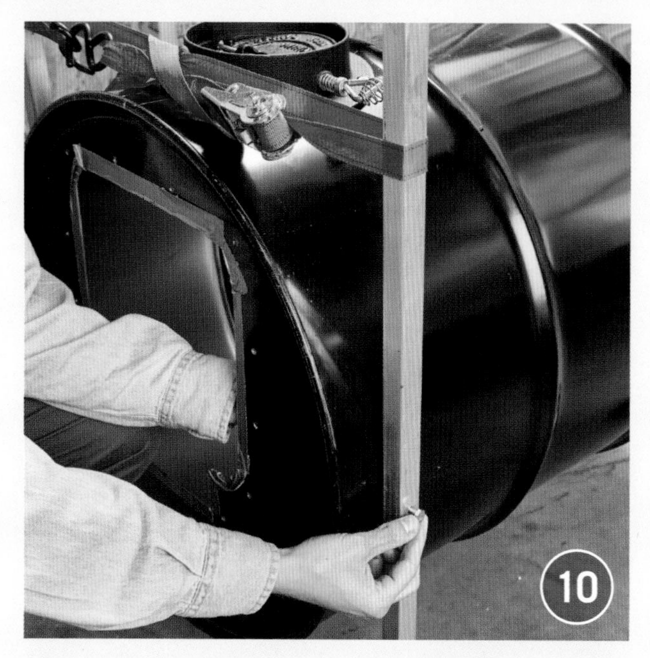

Set the lower barrel onto both frame assemblies and position it so the flue collar is pointing straight up and is level across the top. Strap clamps may help hold the pieces together as you do this. Make sure the uprights are parallel to the barrel ends, then drill a ¼" hole through each upright and into the barrel at its center. Secure the uprights to the barrel with 1½" bolts with washers and nuts. Reach through the door opening to install the washers and nuts inside the barrel.

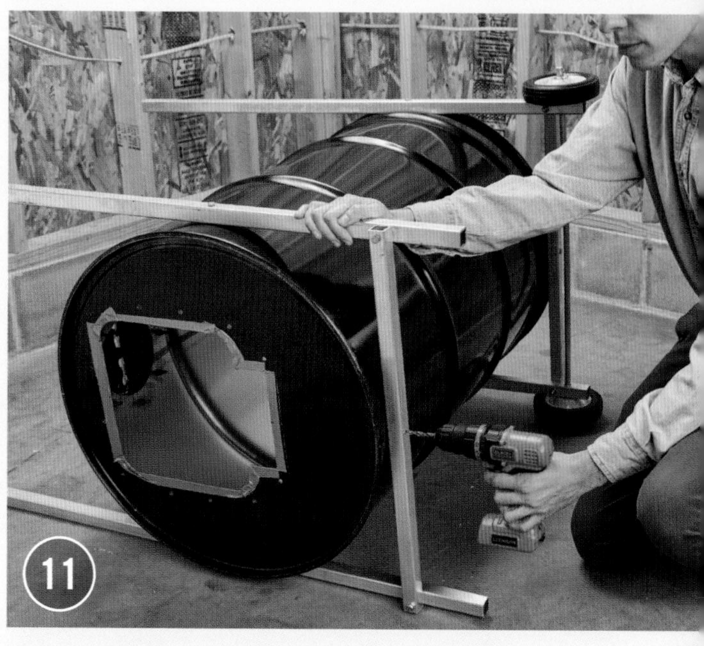

Lay the assembly on its side. Drill a ¼" hole through each lower cross piece and into the bottom center of the barrel. Secure each joint with a 1½" bolt. Stand the assembly back upright.

Cut a piece of 4" flue pipe to extend through the flues. Slide the flue pipe into the flue on the top of the lower barrel, then carefully position the upper barrel onto the frame cross-piece so the flue slides over the flue pipe. Support the top barrel with scraps of lumber.

Measure between the two flue collars to get a starting dimension for the flue pipe. Remove the upper barrel. Measure the depth that the flue pipe will extend into each flange and add both measurements to the first dimension. Cut the flue pipe to the total calculated length, using metal snips or a jigsaw.

Fit the flue pipe onto the flue collar on the bottom barrel and secure it in place with high-temperature silicone caulk. Reposition the barrels in the frame, blocking the upper barrel in place with scrap wood.

Outline the frame opening for the lid on the upper barrel using a straightedge. The bottom edge of the lid should be about 1" above the uprights, and the sides of the lid should be about 4" in from the sides of the barrel. The top of the lid should run along the exact top of the barrel.

Remove the upper barrel. Drill a ½" starter hole just inside the lid opening outline, then cut out the opening with a jigsaw; the cut-out piece will become the smoke chamber lid. Smooth the cut edges of the barrel and the lid with a grinder and abrasive disc. Cover the cut metal edges with duct tape to protect them.

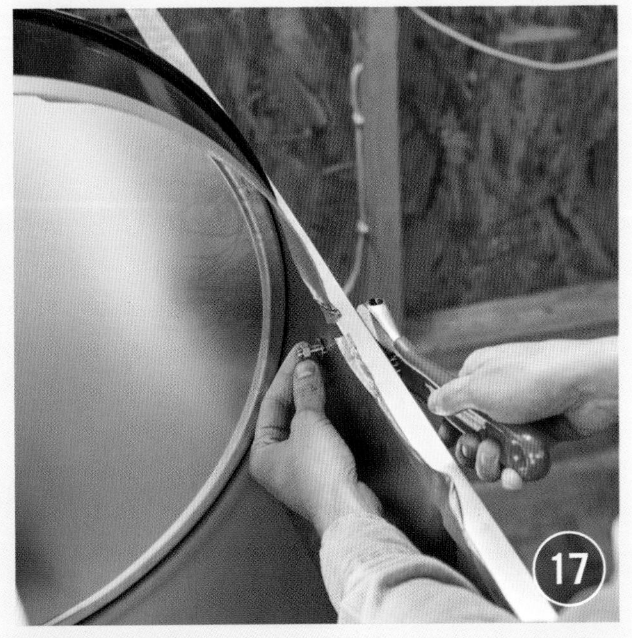

Reposition the upper barrel on the frame, sliding the flue flange over the flue pipe and blocking the barrel in place with wood scraps. Make sure the upper barrel is level. Position the frame angles over the frame rights, then join the frame pieces to the upper barrel by drilling ¼" holes and securing each joint with a 2½" bolt, with a washer and nut on the inside of the barrel. The threaded bolt end will protrude about 1" into the chamber to serve as a support for the cooking grate(s). *(continued)*

Seal the flue pipe joint inside the upper barrel with high-temperature silicone caulk.

Add two more bolts on each side of the barrel, running through the angle and into the barrel interior. Position these so they will support the inside ends of the cooking grate.

Begin adding 1½"-wide strips of sheet aluminum along all four edges of the smoke chamber lid. Complete the long edges first, bending the strips to fit snugly over the barrel ridges; shape them by laying them over a barrel ridge and hammering. The strips should overhang the lid edges by ¾". Leave the strips a little long for now; you will trim them to fit as you install them.

Install each lid strip by trimming it to length with metal snips, clamping it in place on the lid, and drilling a ⅛" hole every 3" to 4" for a pop rivet. The top and bottom strips should overhang the sides of the lid by 1½". Apply high-temperature silicone caulk along the edge of the lid, place the strip onto the caulk, and secure the strip with pop rivets, using a rivet tool.

Apply woodstove door gasket rope along the edges of the lid opening, as directed by the manufacturer, using a high-temperature gasket sealant. Let the sealant cure as directed.

Install the lid with two stainless-steel hinges and ¼ × 1" bolts with washers and nuts.

NOTE: Depending on the hinge design, you may need to add sheetmetal shims under the barrel half of the hinge to prevent the lid from binding. We used metal washers as shims.

(continued)

Cut the handle to length from 1¼" dowel. Drill a ¼" hole about 3" to 4" from each end, making sure the holes are perfectly aligned with each other. Drill matching holes in the lid and install the handle with ¼ × 4½" bolts with washers and nuts. Include a washer and nut on both sides of the lid, and on the backside of the handle to create the offset space between the handle and lid. The dowel should stand away from the lid 2¼" to 2½".

Position the grill grate on the bolts inside the top barrel and measure its position on the end of the barrel. Transfer this measurement to the outside of the barrel. Position a 4" crimp collar so its bottom edge is 4" above the grill mark. Trace around the crimp collar to mark the chimney hole. Drill a starter hole and cut out the chimney hole with a jigsaw.

Insert the crimp collar into the chimney hole and bend the flanges down flush against the end of the barrel. Drill pilot holes and secure the crimp collar with sheetmetal screws driven through the outside of the barrel and into the collar flanges. Apply a bead of high-temperature silicone around the outside of the collar to seal it to the barrel. Let the caulk cure as directed.

Install a 4" elbow and 4 × 24" round duct with damper to the crimp collar and secure the joints with sheetmetal screws. Add a removable cap to the chimney to keep out rain.

Install the remaining crosspiece between the ends of the frame angles, using ½" self-tapping sheetmetal screws. Cut the expanded metal shelf to size with a jigsaw. It should fit against the undersides of the top (horizontal) flanges of the angles and touch the upper barrel and the crosspiece. Drill ¼" holes and attach the shelf to the angles with ¼ × ¾" bolts with washers and nuts.

Line the bottoms of both barrels with firebrick, starting with a row in the center and adding a row on each side. The upper barrel can hold six bricks, starting at the right side of the flue pipe. The lower barrel holds nine bricks, but three of them may have to be trimmed to length, using a brickset chisel and a maul.

Remove the duct tape around the firebox door opening and mount the stove door with the provided bolts. Paint the entire smoker (or any parts), if desired, with high-temperature stove paint.

Brick Pizza Oven

If you truly want the best pizza in town, make it at home in your own wood-fired oven. This is not an exaggeration. Most pizza restaurants use electric ovens, which takes them completely out of the running. Pizzerias with wood-fired or even coal-fired ovens may be good, but they can't make their pizza exactly the way you like, and they can't use your own selected ingredients, such as fresh basil and tomatoes from your garden or the bufala mozzarella from your favorite Italian deli. You really can't beat homemade pizza cooked in a wood-fired oven, and you can't begin to get the same flavors in your regular oven.

A pizza oven isn't just the preferred cooker for pizza—it's also the ultimate centerpiece for outdoor entertaining. And it cooks a lot more than pizza. If you want to spellbind your guests with meat instead, grill a bistecca fiorentina on a grate right over the coals, or char some red peppers next to the fire. The even heat radiated from the brick on all sides makes the oven great for baking too.

The brick oven in this project is based on a traditional barrel-dome design and is the easiest type of oven to build. The brick is a high-temperature firebrick that is commonly available at home centers and masonry suppliers. Be sure to use medium-duty firebrick and refractory mortar, as standard types of brick and mortar can't handle the heat of the cooking fire. Before using the oven for cooking, you must heat-cure it by burning progressively hotter fires over a period of five days. This prevents cracking of the masonry when using the oven at high cooking temperatures.

The floor and dome of the oven must be built over a structural base of masonry or other noncombustible material. The base structure shown here consists of concrete block walls topped with 2-inch-thick concrete pavers. The block walls need a solid foundation that resists ground movement. The ideal foundation is an existing concrete slab, such as a concrete patio. If you must build a new foundation, consult the local building department to learn about structural requirements for your project. For the horizontal structure on top of the walls, it's easiest to use a reinforced precast concrete slab from a local supplier. If this is difficult to find or prohibitively expensive, constructing the horizontal top slab from separate pavers works well.

Constructing the oven requires some basic masonry techniques, including cutting brick and block, mixing and applying mortar, and finishing mortar joints. You can learn about these on pages 79, 83, and 104–111. Because masonry materials vary in size, the dimensions of any part of your oven may differ from those given here, and you may need to modify your brick form based on the actual dimensions of your firebrick.

BRICK PIZZA OVEN

TOOLS & MATERIALS

- 2 × 4 lumber for template
- Framing square
- Mortar mixing tub
- Bricklayer's trowel
- 4' level
- Rubber mallet
- Jointing tool
- Square-end trowel
- Circular saw with wood blades and masonry blade
- Jigsaw
- Wooden yardstick or straight board to use as trammel
- Finish nail
- Drill-driver and drill bits
- Brickset chisel
- Maul
- Stiff-bristle brush
- Infrared thermometer
- Standard concrete blocks, 8 × 8 × 16" (15)
- Combination corner concrete blocks, 8 × 8 × 16" (15)
- Half-block concrete blocks, 8 × 8 × 8" (5)
- Type S mortar
- One-coat stucco or surface-bonding cement mix
- Eye and ear protection
- Work gloves
- 2" × 24" concrete paver slabs (4)
- 1½" × 16" steel angle iron (2)
- ¾" × 4 × 8' plywood
- ⅛" × 4 × 8' hardboard
- 1½" coarse-thread drywall screws
- Duct tape
- 9 × 4½ × 2½" medium-duty firebricks (150)
- Refractory mortar
- 3" galvanized chimney flue with cap (I.D.)

CUTTING LIST

KEY	PART	DIMENSIONS	PCS.	MATERIAL
A	Form base	¾ × 28¼ × 38"	1	¾" plywood
B	Form rib	¾ × 28¼ × 13⅜"	3	¾" plywood
C	Form top	⅛ × 38 × 89½"	1	⅛" hardboard

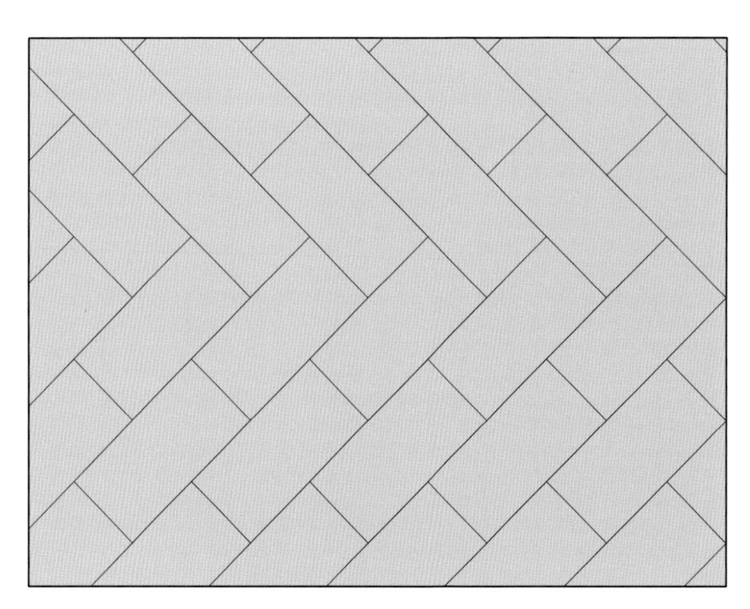

OVEN FLOOR PATTERN

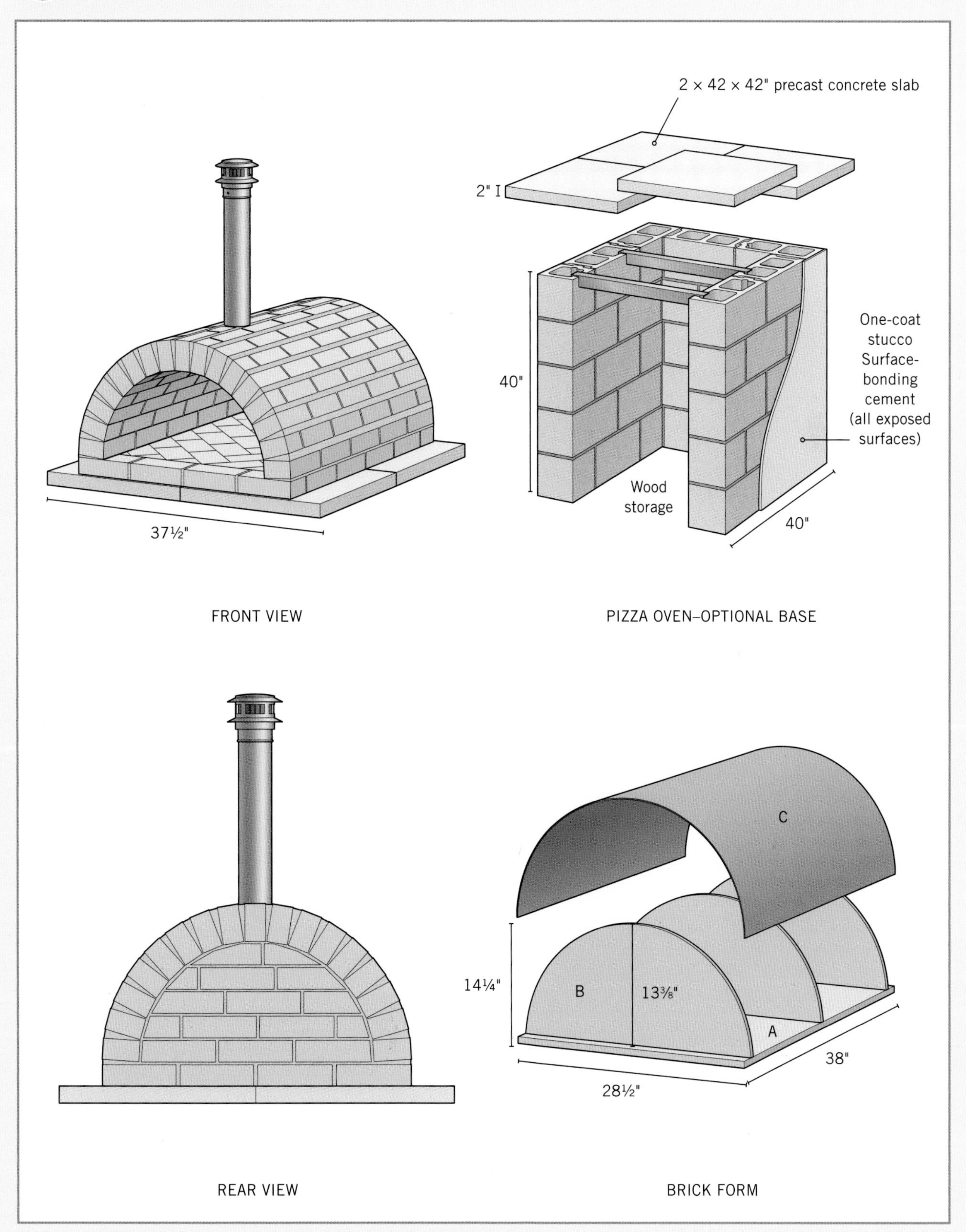

FRONT VIEW

PIZZA OVEN–OPTIONAL BASE

REAR VIEW

BRICK FORM

How to Build the Optional Base

Set the 40" square base for your pizza oven. If you are building your oven on an existing slab, this is simply a matter of outlining the foundation on the slab. But in our example, the oven was being built in the yard. We built a gravel-lined trench according to local building code specifications. **Always check with your local building code office for recommendations on what type of foundation is required.** Build a 2 × 4 guide form to help establish the first course of block, and measure diagonals to make sure the template is square. If the measurements are equal, the outline is square. If not, make small adjustments to square up the template.

Set the first course of concrete block in Type S mortar, following the techniques on pages 104–105. Start one of the side walls with a half block at the front of the base. Complete the course down the first wall, across the rear wall, and up the other side wall, finishing with a corner block. Check the blocks in the first course with a 4' level. All of the blocks should be level with one another in all directions. Use a rubber mallet to tap the blocks to align them. Making the first row level helps ensure that subsequent courses will be level. Once the first course has set, you can remove the guide form.

Set the next courses of block, starting with a corner block at the front of the first wall to create a running bond brick pattern in which the vertical seams are offset. Tool the mortar joints with a jointing tool as you go. Repeat the process to complete the three remaining courses, for a total of five. Tool the joints after every two rows are laid. Let the mortar cure as directed by the manufacturer before moving on to the next step. This will require at least an overnight curing period.

Finish the interior and exterior sides of the block walls with one-coat stucco or surface bonding cement, using a square-end trowel and following the manufacturer's directions. Let the stucco cure as directed.

You will install 16" angle irons across the top row of the foundation to support the front of the concrete pavers and the joint between the first and second row of pavers. Use a circular saw with masonry bit to cut a kerf into the top of the blocks to fit the vertical flange on the angle irons. Set the angle irons in place, then apply a ½"-thick layer of mortar to the tops of the base walls. Set the concrete pavers onto the mortar, and make sure they are level from side to side and front to back. Tool the mortar beneath the edges of the pavers and allow to cure fully—at least overnight.

How to Build the Brick Pizza Oven

Cut the base of the brick form to size from ¾" plywood, using a circular saw. Cut the arching base top to size from ⅛" hardboard.

Draw a semicircle for one of the base ribs using a homemade trammel. Make the trammel by drilling a small hole for a finish nail about 1" from the end of a wooden yardstick or a thin, straight board. Drill another hole 13⅜" away from the first hole. Drive a finish nail through the first hole and into the ¾" plywood, very close to one of the factory (uncut) edges of the panel. Position a pencil in the other hole of the trammel and rotate the trammel to draw the semicircle on the plywood.

Cut out the first rib with a jigsaw. Using the first rib as a template, trace the outlines for two more ribs, then cut them out. Mark three layout lines for the ribs onto both faces of the plywood form base. Locate the two outside lines 3" from each end of the base, and center the third rib in the middle of the base, using a framing square to mark the lines. Center each rib over a line and fasten it to the base with 1½" drywall screws driven through the base and into the edge grain of the rib.

Attach the hardboard form top by fastening it to the side edge of the plywood base, using 1½" drywall screws driven every 4" to 5". The smooth side of the hardboard should face out. Bend the hardboard over the ribs, screwing it down to the ribs as you go. Fasten the hardboard along the other base side, as with the first side.

Begin building the oven by centering the brick form on top of the concrete pavers. Lay a ⅜"-thick bed of refractory mortar and set the first course of firebrick along the base of the form, following the techniques on pages 104–105. In our design, it was possible to use full bricks all the way around the form; however, if your bricks are a slightly different size, you may need to cut some of the bricks. If so, it's best to do this on the back corners, where they will be less visible. Let the mortar cure overnight, then remove the brick form.

(continued)

Dry-lay the firebricks for the oven floor, following the herringbone pattern shown on page 76, or using a different diagonal pattern, if you desire. Cut the bricks to fit along the edges (see page 110), using a circular saw with masonry blade to score the bricks, then breaking them with a brickset chisel and hammer. Fill in the entire floor, then remove the bricks one at a time and set them aside in the same pattern.

Cover the floor area with an even, ⅜"-thick layer of refractory mortar. Set the floor bricks into the mortar in your established pattern. Do not apply mortar between the bricks. Use the 4' level to ensure all the floor bricks are level with one another and with the perimeter bricks. The floor area must be level and smooth, with no raised edges between bricks. Let the mortar cure, at least overnight.

Place the brick form on top of the oven floor so it is centered side to side and front to back. Begin building the oven dome by setting one course of firebrick along the two sides of the oven, staggering the mortar joints with the courses below in an offset, running bond pattern. At the ends of rows, you will need to cut bricks to size with a circular saw and masonry blade. Check your work with a level as you go.

Complete five more courses on each side of the dome, following the same running bond pattern. Because half blocks are not supported by the interior form, you will need to cut small braces to hold the half blocks in place as the dome gets higher. Because of the arching pattern, the joints between bricks will be much wider on the outside of the bricks, while on the inside, the joints will nearly touch. Gradually, you will arch over the top of the form, meeting in the center. As you near the top of the arch, test-fit bricks periodically to ensure that you will meet in the center with full bricks. If you need to begin adjusting the thickness of the mortar lines to ensure a uniform fit, now is the time to do it. *(continued)*

Lay the brick for the last two courses to complete the dome. Start with a half brick at the front, then leave a 3½" space before resuming the running bond pattern for the remainder of both courses. The space is an opening for the chimney.

Install the metal chimney flue so it is centered over the hole in the dome and perfectly plumb. Pack refractory mortar around the chimney to hold it in place. Let the mortar for the chimney and dome cure for two days or as directed by the mortar manufacturer.

Remove the brick form. This may require prying and cutting away pieces of the form in order to extract it. Begin by knocking loose the ribs, then pry away the hardboard arch. Finish by prying out the base of the form. Now, enclose the rear of the oven with courses of firebrick. You will need to cut some small angled pieces of brick at the edges. Let the mortar cure for two days.

Clean the entire oven inside and out with water and a stiff-bristle brush to remove all loose mortar and other debris. If mortar is resisting removal use a diluted muriatic acid solution, following the manufacturer's directions. Let the mortar cure for seven days. The oven does not need to stay dry for this period.

Heat-cure the oven by burning gradually larger fires on the center of the oven floor for a period of five days following the schedule shown below. Monitor the temperature during each firing using an infrared thermometer. Aim the thermometer at the center of the dome interior, directly above the fire.

FIRING SCHEDULE

Burn the fire for at least 6 hours each day, maintaining the correct temperature for that day, as shown in this schedule. Use only hardwood firewood, not sappy wood (such as pine) or charcoal briquettes. Keep the fires small, just large enough to maintain the target temperature. The flames should not reach the oven dome. Do not exceed the target temperature. After five days of firing, you can begin burning fires hot enough to cook pizza, approximately 700° to 800° as measured on the oven floor.

DAYS	TARGET TEMPERATURE
1	300°
2	350°
3	400°
4	450°
5	500°

GRILLING & OUTDOOR COOKING

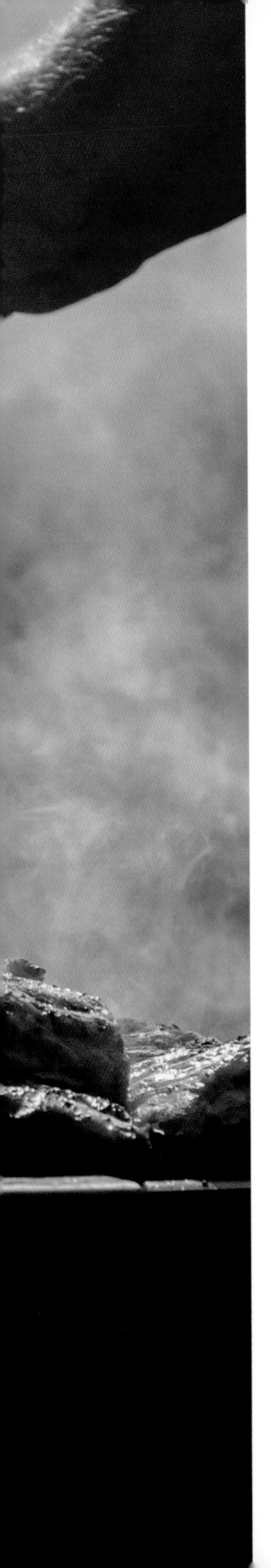

Build & Cook Like a Professional Pit Master

The most popular form of outdoor cooking across the country remains plain old grilling. That's because it's both easy and quick. Follow a few basic rules and you can grill anything to perfection. Of course, you'll need the right equipment, and that's where this section comes in.

Crafting a grill can be a big undertaking or a simple Saturday project, depending on the size you need and how permanent you want the grill to be. You can recycle a steel barrel into a wonderfully long-lasting unit with just a few tools and some metalworking instructions (page 151). Or build a showpiece for your backyard patio out of bricks and mortar (pages 102–07), keeping in mind that it won't be movable once you're done, so plan carefully.

Big or small, metal or mortar, a backyard grill is ideally paired with surfaces, storage and other accessories that can make grilling meals easier, quicker, and more enjoyable. For instance, a **Pitmaster's Locker** like the one on page 126 is perfect for holding bagged charcoal, small tools, and other grilling essentials. It gives you a place to keep your grilling tools and equipment safe from critters and the elements, and generally keeps your grilling area organized and tidy.

Put together the **Patio Prep Cart** on page 120 and you'll have plenty of room to spread out, with a place for every dish you cook and every ingredient you need. Because one thing most grillers quickly learn: you never have enough prep room. There's always some plate of food, or cutting board full of meat that just doesn't fit anywhere nearby.

Take the idea of extra storage and prep space to its logical extreme and you will start thinking about creating a true outdoor kitchen. The kind of structures outlined on pages 112–119 are best if you live in a warm climate and tend to spend close to half the year entertaining, eating or just relaxing outside.

TOOLS & MATERIALS

- Wheelbarrow
- Landscape paint
- String and stakes
- Spades
- Metal pipe
- Landscape edging
- Level
- Garden rake
- Plate vibrator
- Metal fireplace liner
- Compactible gravel
- Top-dressing rock or gravel
- Wall stones
- Eye and ear protection
- Work gloves

Fire Pit Rotisserie

This project can be very easy if you already have a fire pit—a matter of simply adding a purchased add-on rotisserie spit to an existing fire pit that you have in your yard. But we've also included complete instructions for building a great fire pit and safety pad from scratch. You can adapt this project to whatever circumstances are found in your yard.

Rotisserie spits are available in many styles, from hand-cranked units to those with solar-powered motors to turn the spit. And they come in several different sizes, some appropriate to slow-cooking whole chickens or turkeys, others large enough to handle small goats or pigs. For most backyard fire pits, though, a 48- or 52-inch spit that just spans the fire pit itself is the best choice.

A fire pit with rotisserie can become a focal point and gathering spot for backyard entertaining and dining. The fire pit features here is constructed around a 36-inch corrugated metal liner, but you could also build it with a commercially available fire pit bowl or other enclosure available on any home center. We have surrounded the fire pit liner with cut limestone slabs, but this is just one option. Clay bricks, fire bricks, and retaining wall blocks are among other materials that could be used to build the surrounding walls.

Make sure to check with your local code for stipulations on the allowable size and location of your fire pit. For example, most municipalities have rules regarding how far a fire pit must be set back from fences or wooden structures in order to remain safe. Some localities may not allow outdoor burning at all.

The rotisserie spit kit we've chosen is typical for installation. This one happens to use a battery-operated motor for wireless convenience, but corded electric units and solar-powered units install in much the same way across all manufacturers. The upright support poles can be left in place permanently, or they can be removed after each use. But the horizontal spit and motor unit should be removed and stored away after each use to extend its life.

Some pointers to consider when using your fire pit: 1) Make sure there are no bans in effect; 2) Evaluate wind conditions and avoid building a fire if winds are heavy and/or blowing toward your home; 3) Keep shovels, sand, water, and a fire extinguisher nearby; 4) Extinguish fire with water and never leave the fire pit unattended.

CROSS SECTION: FIRE PIT

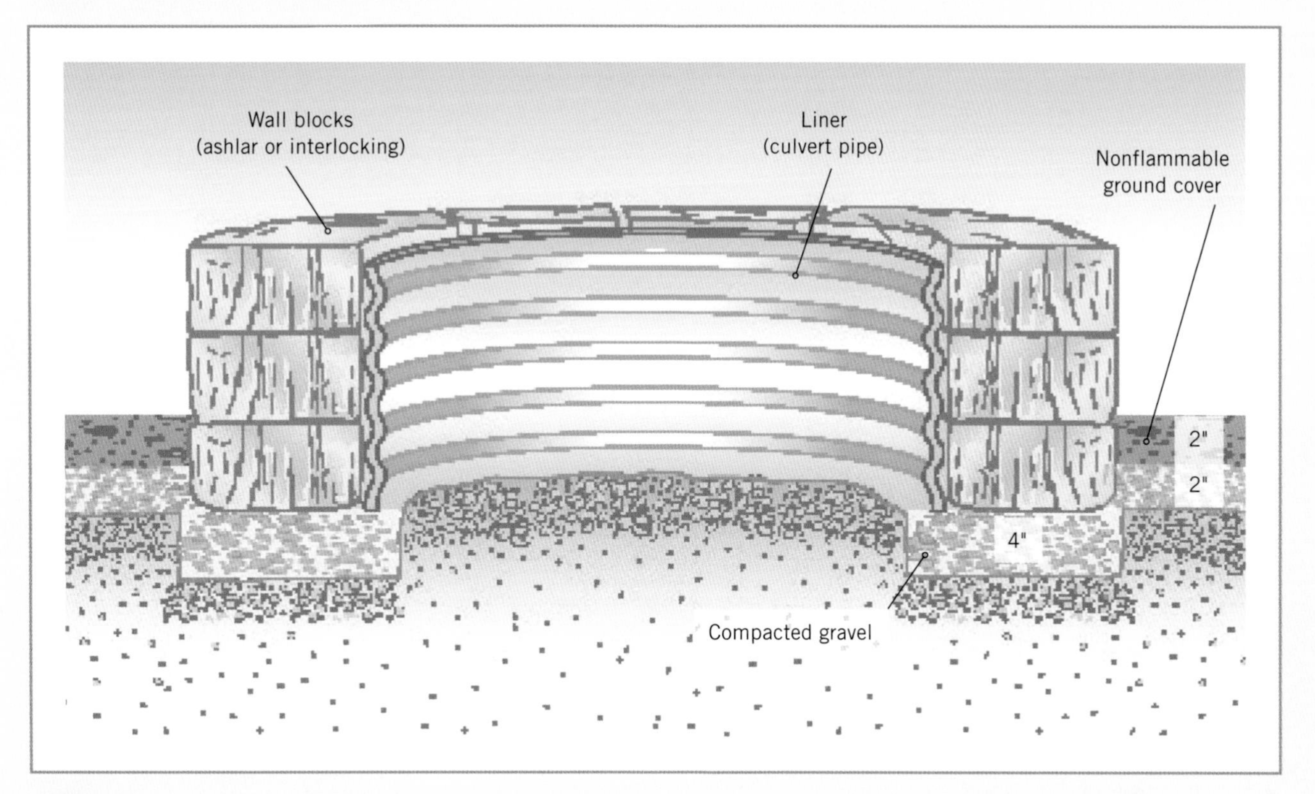

PLAN VIEW: FIRE PIT

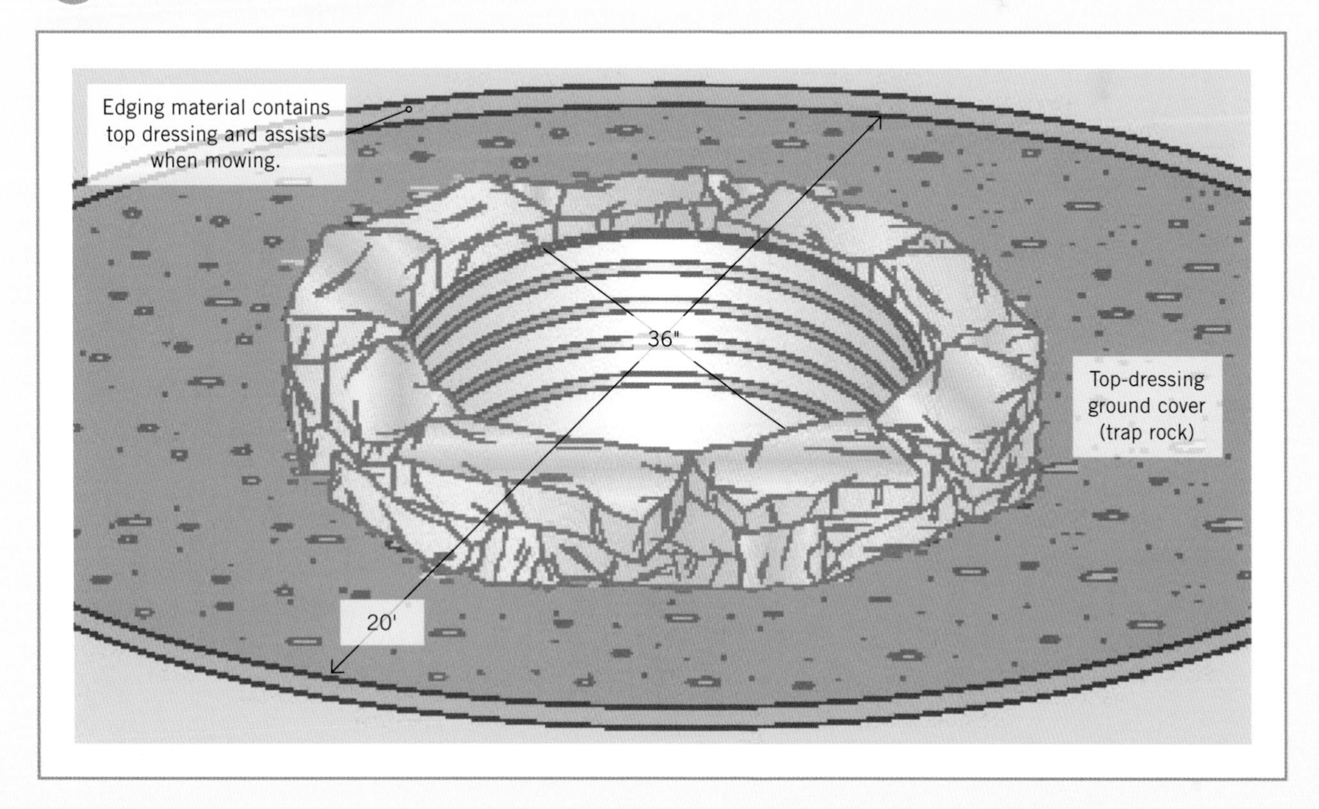

How to Build the Fire Pit

Outline the location for your fire pit and the fire pit safety area by drawing concentric circles with landscape paint, using a string and pole for guidance.

Remove a 4"-deep layer of sod and dirt in the fire pit and safety areas (the depth of excavation depends on what materials you're installing in the safety zone).

Dig a 4"-deep trench for the perimeter stones that will ring the liner pit.

Fill the trench for the perimeter stones with compactible gravel and tamp thoroughly. Then scatter gravel to within 2½" of the paver edging throughout the project area. It is not necessary to tamp this layer at this time.

Place your metal fire ring so it is level on the gravel layer and centered around the center pipe.

Arrange the first course of wall blocks around the fire ring. Keep gaps even and check with a level, adding or removing gravel as needed.

Install the second course of wall block, taking care to evenly stagger the vertical joints on the first and second courses. Add the remaining courses to the desired height.

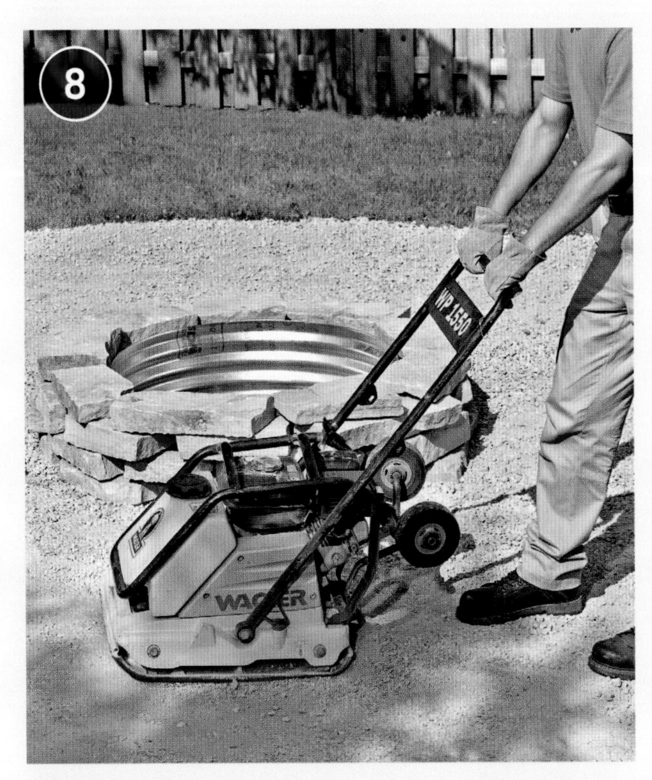

Compact the gravel in the seating/safety area using a rental plate vibrator.

Place and compact a later of top-dressing rock in the seating/ safety area to complete the fire pit.

How to Add the Rotisserie to the Fire Pit

Choose a location for the two upright support posts. The span between the posts depends on the kit you buy, but typically you would seek to place the uprights as close to the inside edges of the fire pit as you can. These posts will get very hot, and it's a good ideal to keep them inside within the boundaries of the fire pit. With a mallet, drive the blunt ends of the posts down into the ground, taking care to keep them perfectly plumb.

Insert the motor head bracket onto the larger-diameter support post. The head should be installed so the thumb latch on top of the motor head bracket faces upward. To adjust the height up or down, squeeze the thumb latch, slide the bracket to the desired height, and release the thumb latch to fix the motor in place.

To install the motor, locate the motor support slots located on the outside of the motor support bracket. Insert the bottom of the motor mounting tabs into the top of the slots and push the motor down into position. Take care not to install the motor upside down.

Begin assembly of the handle unit by sliding the outboard support clamp onto the smaller support post so the U-shaped cutout faces upward. Adjusting height is done by squeezing the tabs on the clap and sliding the clamp up or down on the support post.

Slide the thumbscrew bushing onto the threaded end of the spit rod rust past the threads. Screw down the thumbscrew tightly.

Place the looped end of the counterbalance over the threads on the spit rod and against the lock nut on the bushing.

Thread the handle onto the spit rod. Insert the spit rod into the motor assembly on the opposite post. Tighten the bushing thumbscrew down to lock it in place.

Even weight distribution is critical in rotisserie cooking, and here is where the counterbalance comes in. Once a food item is secured in the prongs on the spit rod, find the heaviest side of the food, then manually turn the rod until this heaviest portion is facing up. Allow the counterweight to point straight downward, and secure the handle to hold it in place. This will allow the spit to be relatively balanced so the motor can function smoothly. As the food item cooks and shrinks, you can expect to readjust the counterweight several times.

Barrel Grill

A barrel grill isn't just a funky adaptation of a common material; barrels actually make darned good grills. They're big, they're durable, and they're just the right shape for naturally circulating heat around the food. Barrel grills are suitable for charcoal fires and even wood fires with decent-size logs. As for cooking area, a 55-gallon barrel yields about 750 square inches of cooking surface. You'd be hard-pressed to find a commercial charcoal grill with that kind of capacity.

As a popular conversion project, barrel grills have inspired a lot of custom designs, with various stands, barrel configurations, and construction techniques. Some require welding, some use parts from more than one barrel, and some include a chimney or other extra features. The version shown here is adapted from some of the simplest design ideas out there and may be the easiest barrel grill to build (or one of the easiest). It's a single-barrel, no-weld design that uses only three main parts: a 55-gallon barrel, two sticks of angle iron, and a sheet of expanded metal, plus a handful of bolts.

Building this grill works best when you cut the barrel with a grinder and a cutoff disc. This allows you to keep the steel rims along the heads of the barrel intact so they can serve as stops for the side edges of the lid. Alternatively, you can use a jigsaw to make the cuts (cutting just inside the rim) and add bolts to stop the lid in the closed position.

Use a *tight head*, or *closed head*, barrel (with permanently attached heads) made of plain carbon steel or stainless steel. Do not use a galvanized barrel, as the galvanized coating burns at high heat, releasing toxic fumes. Also make sure the barrel is *unlined*. Some barrels have a plastic lining or coating on the interior that releases toxic fumes when burned.

WARNING: Remove all bungs (threaded plugs in the barrel heads) before drilling, cutting, or grinding any part of a barrel. If the bungs are not removed, heated air trapped inside the barrel can cause the barrel to explode.

TOOLS & MATERIALS

- 55-gallon unlined steel barrel (1)
- 3" stainless-steel hinges (2)
- 3⁄16 × ½" stainless-steel flathead stove bolts with washers and nuts (12)
- ¼ × 2½" stainless-steel flathead stove bolts with washers and nuts (2)
- 1"-diameter stainless-steel fender washers (with ¼" hole) (2)
- ¼ × 1½" stainless-steel flathead stove bolts (12) with washers (24) and nuts (12); add ¼ × 1½" stainless-steel flathead stove bolts (4), washers (8), and nuts (4) (optional; for warming shelf)
- ¼ × 3" stainless-steel flathead stove bolts (2) with washers and nuts (6)
- 1 × 1 × 96" aluminum angle pieces (2)
- 2 × 4' aluminum or plain steel expanded metal sheet or repurposed grill grates (1)
- 1¼"-diameter × 6" to 8" hardwood dowel
- 1"-diameter disc magnets (6) (optional)
- Eye protection
- Heavy-duty work gloves
- Framing square
- Marker
- Straightedge
- Drill-driver
- 3⁄16", ¼", and ¾" drill bits or step bit
- Grinder with metal-cutting and abrasive grinding discs
- Flat pry bar
- Adjustable wrench or socket wrench
- Eye and ear protection
- Work gloves

How to Build the Barrel Grill

Draw perpendicular reference lines on one end of the barrel: Use a framing square and a marker to draw a straight line across the barrel end at its widest point, drawing the line through the center of the circle. Measure the length of the line and mark its center. Place the square on the line at the center mark and draw a second line perpendicular to the first line.

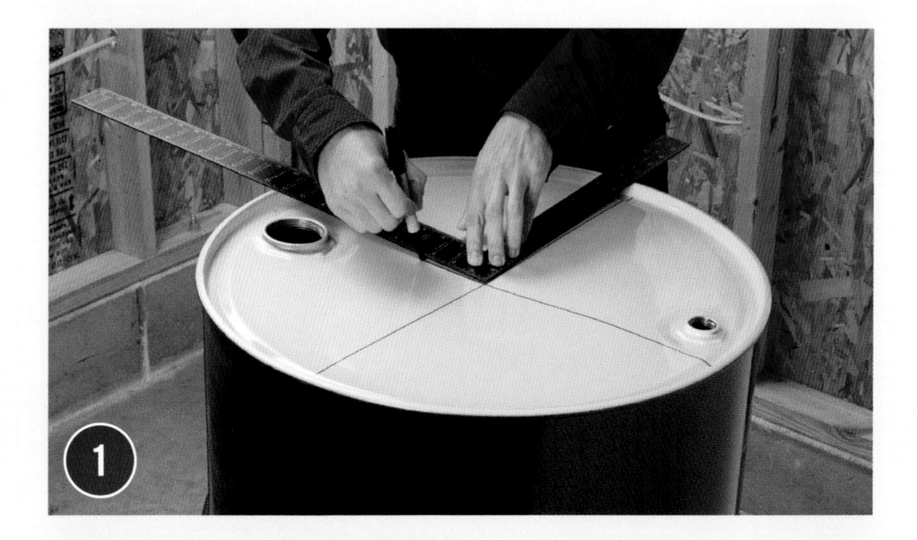

Transfer the reference lines to the other end of the barrel by placing the square over the end of the barrel and continuing one of the reference lines along the side of the barrel; this line will also serve as the cutting line for the bottom edge of the lid. Draw two perpendicular reference lines on the other end of the barrel, matching the first barrel end.

Draw the cutting line for the top of the lid by making at mark at both ends of the barrel, 1" from the reference line adjacent to the bottom lid cutting line. The lid is 1" larger than ¼ of the barrel's circumference. Use a straightedge or the framing square to draw the top lid cutting line between the marks.

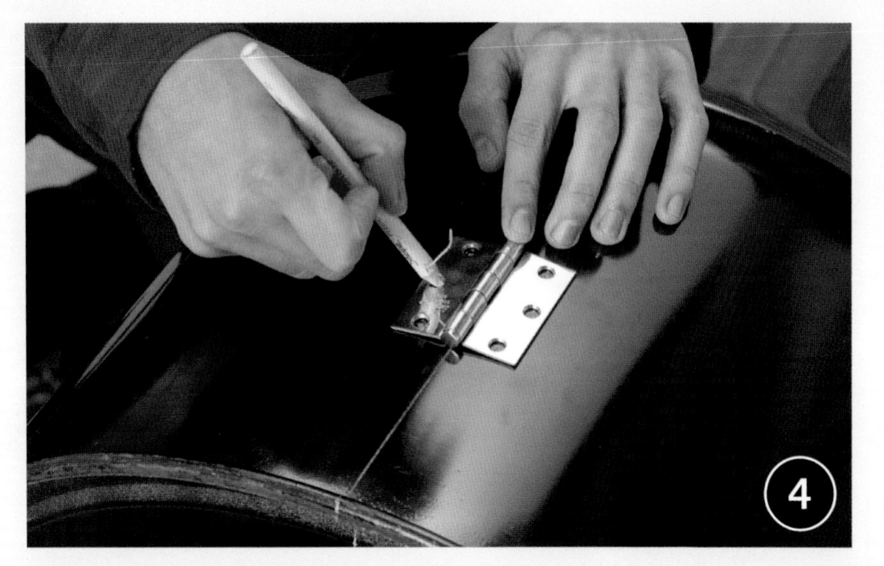

Mark the screw holes for the lid hinges by placing each hinge so it is centered over the top lid cutting line and tracing inside the hinge's screw holes. Drill a 3⁄16" hole through the side of the barrel at each mark.

WARNING: Remove all plugs covering the bung holes of the barrel to prevent a dangerous buildup of pressure when drilling or cutting into any part of the barrel. Wear safety goggles and work gloves when drilling and cutting metal.

Cut out the lid using a grinder with a metal-cutting disc. When cutting the ends of the lid (along the rim of the barrel head), work carefully so that you cut through only the outer wall of the barrel, leaving the steel rim under the wall intact. After making the cuts, separate the lid from the rims with a small flat pry bar. Smooth all of the cut edges on the barrel and the lid with the grinder and an abrasive disc.

Prepare the grill legs by marking the center of two 8'-long pieces of 1" aluminum angle. Cut through one flange of the angle at the mark, leaving the other flange intact. Bend the angle—opening up the cut—so the two legs form a 40° angle.

(continued)

Fasten a leg pair to each end of the barrel. At the top of the legs, drill a ¼" hole through the barrel end and secure the legs with a ¼ × 2½" bolt, with a 1" fender washer on the outside of the legs and a standard washer and nut on the inside of the barrel. Fasten each leg near the lower edge of the barrel by drilling through the leg flange and the barrel and securing the leg with a ¼ × 1½" bolt, with washers and nuts (nuts go on the inside of the barrel). Tighten all nuts with an adjustable wrench or ratchet wrench.

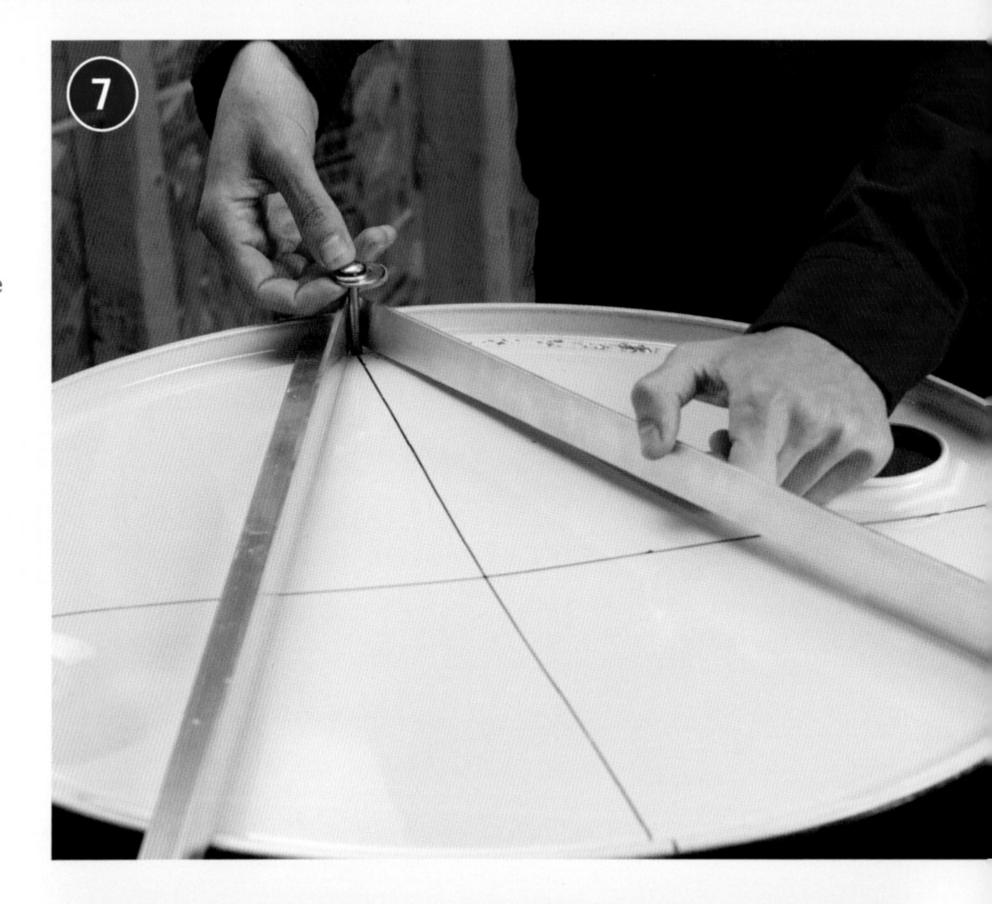

Add the support bolts on each end of the barrel for the grates and optional warming shelf, as shown on page 97. Drill ¼" holes and install a ¼ × 1½" bolt with washers and a nut (on barrel interior) in each hole, as follows: two holes for the cooking grate 1" below the horizontal reference line; two holes for the coal grate, 5" to 6" below the cooking grate level; two holes for the optional warming shelf, about 5¼" above the cooking grate level. Also drill three ¾" ventilation holes, evenly spaced, about 2" below the coal grate location.

NOTE: If your cooking or coal grate happens to fit the barrel at a different location, simply modify the bolt locations as needed so you don't have to cut down the grate to fit.

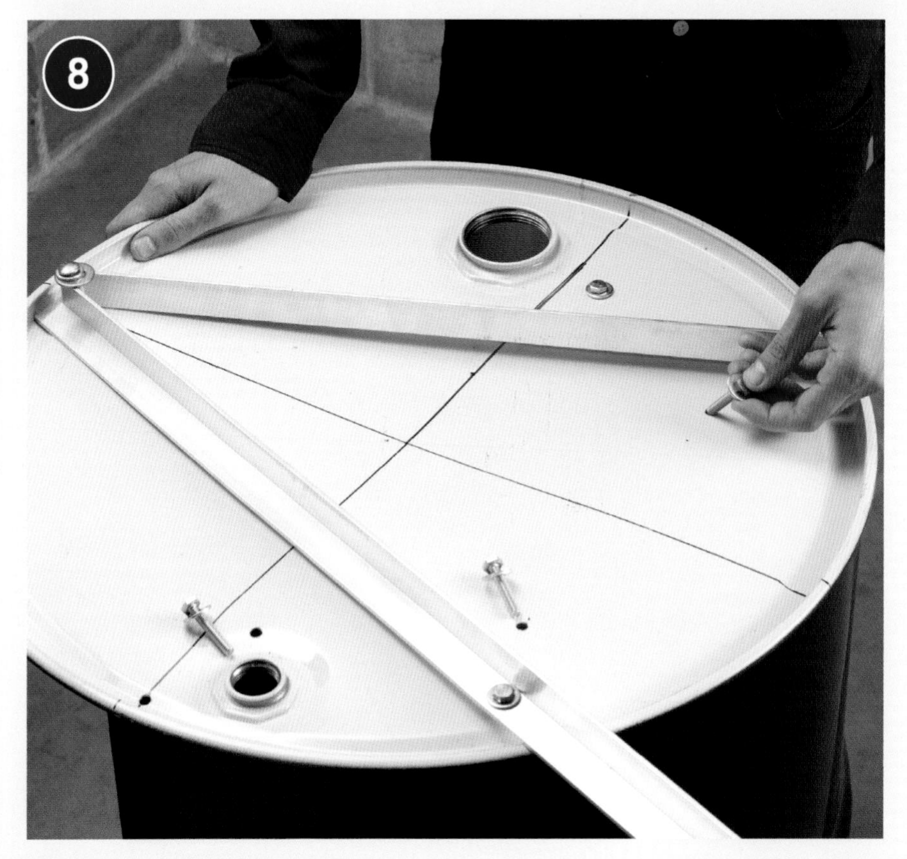

Cut the cooking grate, coal grate, and warming shelf grate (as applicable) to fit, using the grinder or a jigsaw. Remove any sharp edges with the grinder and abrasive disc. Set the grates onto the support bolts in the grill.

Install the lid with the hinges and 3⁄16 × ½" bolts, with a washer and nut on the barrel interior. Create a handle with a 6" to 8" length of hardwood dowel and two ¼" × 3" stove bolts. Include a washer and nut on the inside of the handle and on both sides of the lid.

TIP: Use 1"-diameter magnets to cover the ventilation holes in the barrel ends. The magnets get hot when the fire's going, so be sure to move them with tongs or heatproof grill gloves.

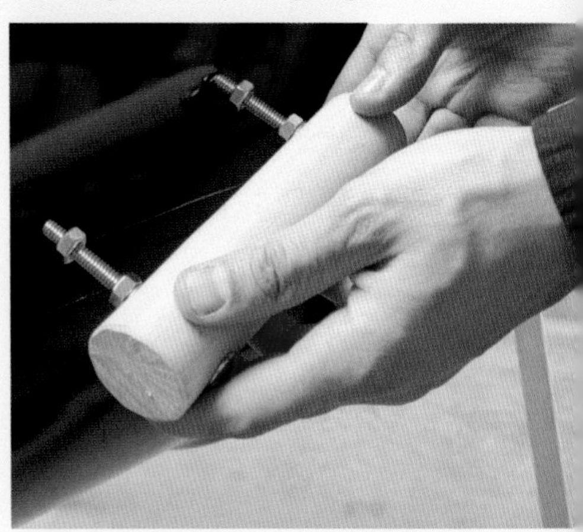

Brick Barbecue Grill

The barbecue design shown here is constructed with double walls—an inner wall made of heat-resistant fire brick set on edge surrounding the cooking area, and an outer wall made of engineer brick. We chose this brick because its larger dimensions mean you'll have fewer bricks to lay. You'll need to adjust the design if you select another brick size. A 4-inch air space between the walls helps insulate the cooking area. The walls are capped with thin pieces of cut stone.

Refractory mortar is recommended for use in areas of direct fire contact. It is heat resistant and the joints will last a long time without cracking. Ask a local brickyard to recommend a refractory mortar for outdoor use.

The foundation combines a 12-inch-deep footing supporting a reinforced slab. This structure, known as a floating footing, is designed to shift as a unit when temperature changes cause the ground to shift. Ask a building inspector about local Building Code specifications.

TOOLS & MATERIALS

Tape measure
Hammer
Brickset chisel
Mason's string
Shovel
Aviation snips
Reciprocating saw or hacksaw
Masonry hoe
Shovel
Wood float
Chalk line
Level
Wheelbarrow
Mason's trowel
Jointing tool
Garden stakes
2 × 4 lumber
18-gauge galvanized metal mesh
#4 rebar
16-gauge tie wire
Bolsters
Fire brick (4½ × 2½ × 9")
Engineer brick (4 × 3⅕ × 8")
Type N or Type S mortar
⅜"-dia. dowel
Metal ties
4" tee plates
Engineer brick (4 × 2 × 12")
Brick sealer
Stainless-steel expanded mesh (23¾ × 30")
Cooking grills (23⅜ × 15½")
Ash pan
Concrete mix

MORTAR DATA

Type N Mortar: Non-structural mortar for veneer applications, reaches 750 psi @ 28 days

Type S Mortar: Structural mortar for veneer structural applications, exceeds 1,800 psi @ 28 days

POURING A FLOATING FOOTING

Lay out a 4 × 5' area. Dig a continuous trench 12" wide × 10" deep along the perimeter of the area, leaving a rectangular mound in the center. Remove 4" of soil from the top of the mound, and round over the edges. Set a 2 × 4 form around the site so that the top is 2" above the ground along the back and 1½" above the ground along the front. This slope will help shed water. Reinforce the footing with five 52"-long pieces of rebar. Use a mason's string and a line level to ensure that the forms are level from side to side. Set the rebar on the bolster 4" from the front and rear sides of the trench, centered from side to side. Space the remaining three bars evenly in between. Coat the forms with vegetable oil or release agent, and pour the concrete.

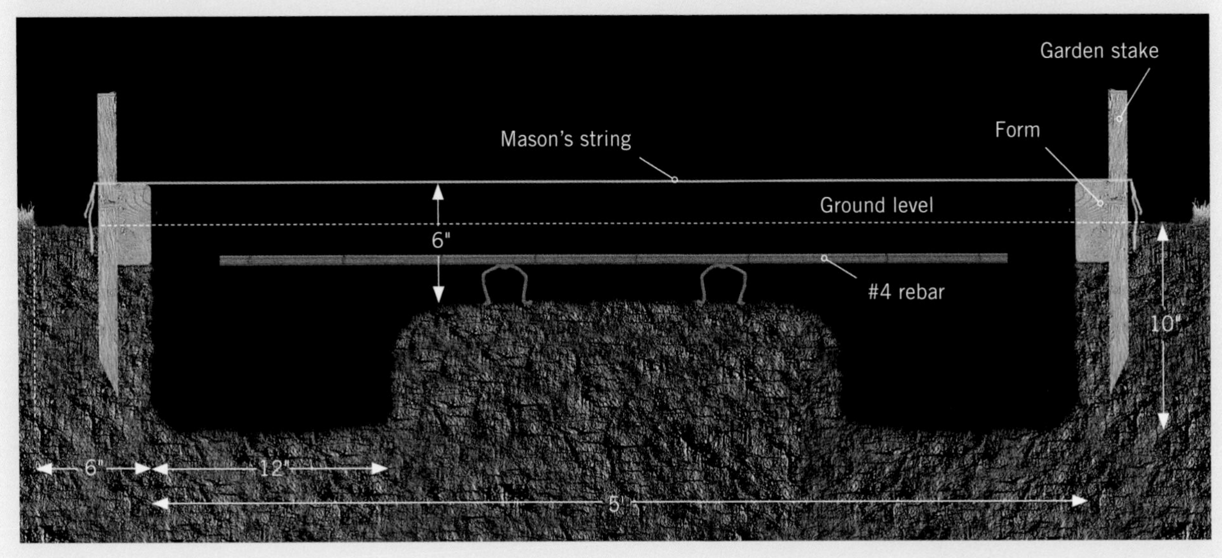

How to Build the Brick Barbecue

After the footing has cured for one week, use a chalk line to mark the layout for the inner edge of the fire brick wall. Make a line 4" in from the front edge of the footing and a center line perpendicular to the first line. Make a 24 × 32" rectangle that starts at the 4" line and is centered on the center line.

Dry-lay the first course of fire brick around the outside of the rectangle, allowing for ⅛"-thick mortar joints.

NOTE: Proper placement of the inner walls is necessary so they can support the grills. Start with a full brick at the 4" line to start the right and left walls. Complete the course with a cut brick in the middle of the short wall.

Dry-lay the outer wall, as shown here, using 4 × 3⅕ × 8" nominal engineer brick. Gap the bricks for ⅜" mortar joints. The rear wall should come within ⅜" of the last fire brick in the left inner wall. Complete the left wall with a cut brick in the middle of the wall. Mark reference lines for this outer wall.

Make a story pole. On one side, mark 8 courses of fire brick, leaving a ⅜" gap for the bottom mortar joint and ⅛" gaps for the remaining joints. The top of the final course should be 36" from the bottom edge. Transfer the top line to the other side of the pole. Lay out 11 courses of engineer brick, spacing them evenly so that the final course is flush with the 36" line. Each horizontal mortar joint will be slightly less than ½" thick.

Lay a bed of mortar for a ⅜" joint along the reference lines for the inner wall, then lay the first course of fire brick, using ⅛" joints between the bricks.

Lay the first course of the outer wall, using Type N or Type S mortar. Use oiled ⅜" dowels to create weep holes behind the front bricks of the left and right walls. Alternate laying the inner and outer walls, checking your work with the story pole and a level after every course.

(continued)

Start the second course of the outer wall using a half-brick butted against each side of the inner wall, then complete the course. Because there is a half-brick in the right outer wall, you need to use two three-quarter bricks in the second course to stagger the joints.

Place metal ties between the corners of the inner and outer walls, at the second, third, fifth, and seventh courses. Use ties at the front junctions and along the rear walls. Mortar the joint where the left inner wall meets the rear outer wall.

Smooth the mortar joints with a jointing tool when the mortar has hardened enough to resist minimal finger pressure. Check the joints in both walls after every few courses. The different mortars may need smoothing at different times.

Add tee plates for grill supports above the fifth, sixth, and seventh courses. Use 4"-wide plates with flanges that are no more than 3⁄32" thick. Position the plates along the side fire brick walls, centered 3", 12", 18", and 27" from the rear fire brick wall.

When both walls are complete, install the capstones. Lay a bed of Type N or Type S mortar for a 3⁄8"-thick joint on top of the inner and outer walls. Lay the capstone flat across the walls, keeping one end flush with the inner face of the fire brick. Make sure the bricks are level, and tool the joints when they are ready. After a week, seal the capstones and the joints between them with brick sealer and install the grills.

TIPS FOR WORKING WITH MORTAR

Remove wet mortar from joints in natural stone walls using a jointer or even piece of wood. By raking out ½" or so of mortar you will create a wall with subtle shadow lines between stones instead of tooled mortar, which can look a bit out of place with irregular stone.

Blend liquid stucco and mortar pigment with the mixing water before adding to the dry mortar mix. Add the same amount of color and water to each batch for color consistency.

Working with Mortar

Working with brick and block is a satisfying process: with each unit that is added, the project grows and its appearance improves. Whether you're building a block retaining wall, a brick barbeque, or paving a walk with mortared brick, you're sure to enjoy the project as well as its results.

Brick and block provide a sense of balance as well as color and texture to your home and landscape. Structures built with these materials are attractive, durable, and low maintenance.

Careful planning and a thoughtful design will help you build a project that makes sense for your home, your yard, and your budget. Projects are simpler to build if you create a design that limits the number of masonry units that must be cut.

Brick and decorative block colors, styles, and textures vary widely by region, reflecting regional trends. Choose a color and style that complements the style of your home and yard as well as the region in which you live. Colors and styles are often discontinued abruptly, so it's a good idea to buy a few extra units to have on hand for repairs.

TIP

Laying brick and block is a precise business. Many of the tools necessary for these projects relate to establishing and maintaining true, square, and level structures, while others relate to cutting the masonry units and placing the mortar. It makes sense to purchase tools you'll use again, but it's more cost effective to rent specialty items, such as a brick splitter.

Tools for Brick & Block Projects

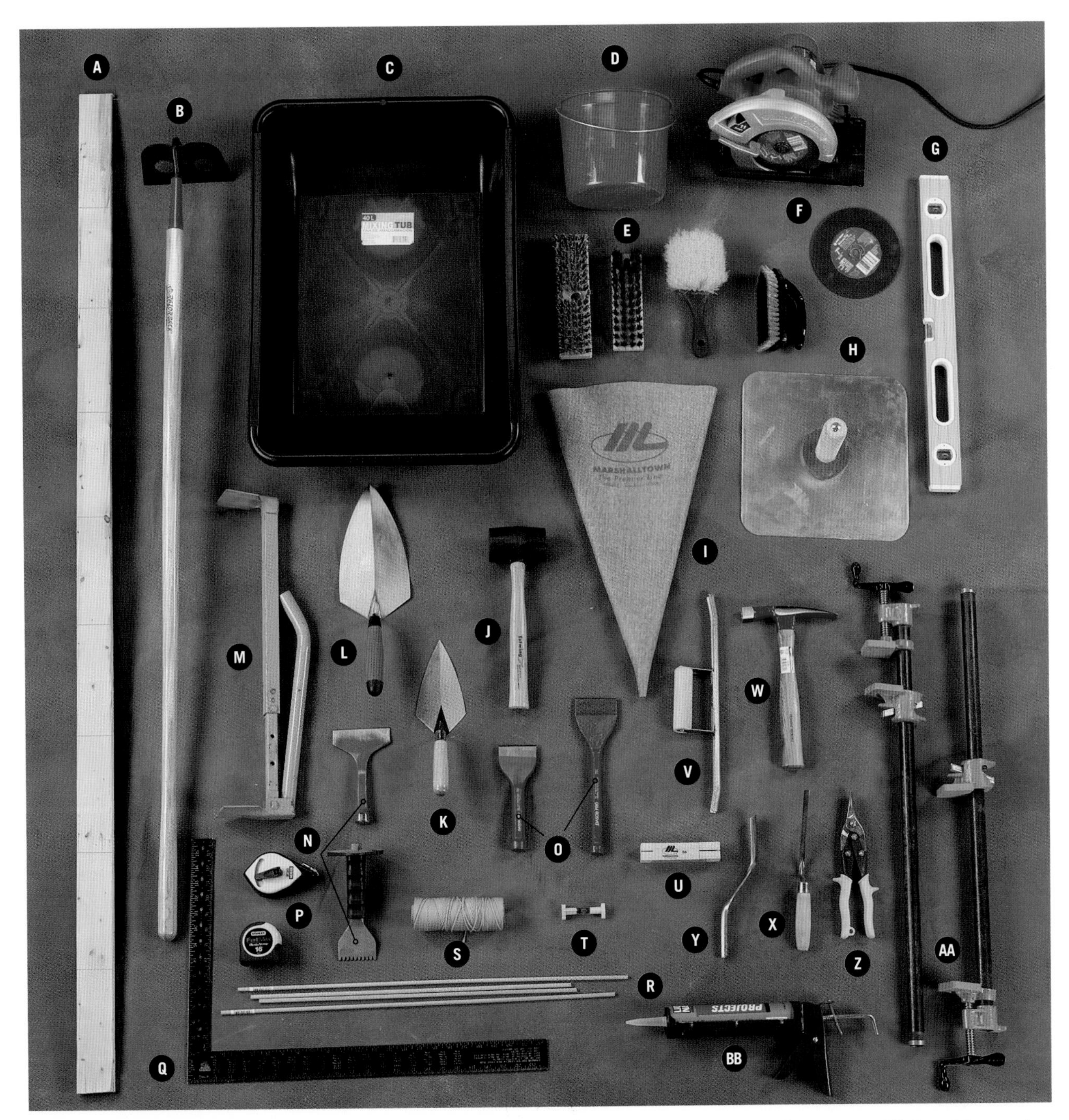

Mason's tools include a story pole (A) for checking stacked masonry units; masonry hoe (B) and mortar box (C) for mixing mortar; a bucket (D) and stiff bristle brushes (E) for removing stains and loose materials; circular saw and masonry-cutting blades (F) for scoring brick and block; level (G) for checking stacked masonry units; mortar hawk (H) for holding mortar; mortar bag (I) for filling horizontal joints; rubber mallet (J) for setting paver stones; pointing trowel (K) for furrowing mortar; London trowel (L) for applying mortar; brick tongs (M) for carrying multiple bricks; brick sets (N) for splitting brick, block, and stone; cold chisels (O) for scoring masonry units; a tape measure and chalk line (P) for marking layout lines on footings or slabs; a framing square (Q) for setting project outlines; ⅜" dowels (R) for spacers between dry-laid masonry units; mason's string (S) and line blocks (T) for stacking brick and block; a line level (U) for making layouts and setting slope; sled jointer (V) for finishing long joints; mason's hammer (W) for chipping brick and stone; tuck pointer (X); S-shaped jointer (Y); aviation snips (Z) for trimming metal ties and lath; pipe clamps (AA) for aligning brick and block to be scored; caulk gun (BB) for sealing around fasteners and house trim.

Tips for Cutting Bricks

How to Score & Cut Brick

Score all four sides of the brick first with a brickset chisel and maul when cuts fall over the web area, and not over the core. Tap the chisel to leave scored cutting marks ⅛ to ¼" deep, then strike a firm final blow to the chisel to split the brick. Properly scored bricks split cleanly with one firm blow.

OPTION: When you need to split a lot of bricks uniformly and quickly, use a circular saw fitted with a masonry blade to score the bricks, then split them individually with a chisel. For quick scoring, clamp them securely at each end with a pipe or bar clamp, making sure the ends are aligned.

REMEMBER: Wear eye protection when using striking or cutting tools.

How to Angle-Cut Brick

Mark the final cutting line on the brick. To avoid ruining the brick, you will need to make gradual cuts until you reach this line. Score a straight line for the first cut in the waste area of the brick about ⅛" from the starting point of the final cutting line, perpendicular to the edge of the brick. Make the first cut.

Keep the chisel stationary at the point of the first cut, pivot it slightly, then score and cut again. It is important to keep the pivot point of the chisel at the edge of the brick. Repeat until all of the waste area is removed.

How to Cut Brick with a Brick Splitter

A brick splitter makes accurate, consistent cuts in bricks and pavers with no scoring required. It is a good idea to rent one if your project requires many cuts. To use the brick splitter, first mark a cutting line on the brick, then set the brick on the table of the splitter, aligning the cutting line with the cutting blade on the tool.

Once the brick is in position on the splitter table, pull down sharply on the handle. The cutting blade on the splitter will cleave the brick along the cutting line. For efficiency, mark cutting lines on several bricks at the same time (see page 110).

How to Cut Concrete Block

Mark cutting lines on both faces of the block, then score ⅛ to ¼"-deep cuts along the lines using a circular saw equipped with a masonry blade.

Use a mason's chisel and maul to split one face of the block along the cutting line. Turn the block over and split the other face.

OPTION: Cut half blocks from combination corner blocks. Corner blocks have preformed cores in the center of the web. Score lightly above the core, then rap with a mason's chisel to break off half blocks.

Outdoor Masonry Kitchen

With its perfect blend of indoor convenience and alfresco atmosphere, it's easy to see why the outdoor kitchen is one of today's most popular home upgrades. In terms of design, outdoor kitchens can take almost any form, but most are planned around the essential elements of a built-in grill and convenient countertop surfaces (preferably on both sides of the grill). Secure storage inside the cooking cabinet is another feature many outdoor cooks find indispensable.

The kitchen design in this project combines all three of these elements in a moderately sized cooking station that can fit a variety of kitchen configurations. The structure is freestanding and self-supporting, so it can go almost anywhere—on top of a patio, right next to a house wall, out by the pool, or out in the yard to create a remote entertainment getaway. Adding a table and chairs or a casual sitting area might be all you need to complete your kitchen accommodations. But best of all, this kitchen is made almost entirely of inexpensive masonry materials.

Concrete and masonry are ideally suited to outdoor kitchen construction. It's noncombustible, not damaged by water, and can easily withstand decades of outdoor exposure. In fact, a little weathering makes masonry look even better. In this project, the kitchen's structural cabinet is built with concrete block on top of a reinforced concrete slab. The countertop is 2-inch-thick poured concrete that you cast in place over two layers of cementboard (for a small kitchen or a standalone island, you might prefer to build a mold-cast countertop). The block sides of the cabinet provide plenty of support for the countertop, as well as a good surface for applying the stucco finish. You could also finish the cabinet with veneer stone or tile.

TOOLS & MATERIALS

- Chalk line
- Pointed trowel
- Masonry mixing tools
- Level
- Mason's string
- Circular saw with masonry blade
- Utility knife
- Straightedge
- Square-notched trowel
- Metal snips
- Wood float
- Steel finishing trowel
- Drill with masonry bit
- Concrete block
- Mortar mix or mason mix
- Metal reinforcement (as required)
- Steel angle iron
- ½" cementboard (two 8'-long sheets)
- 2 × 4 and 2 × 6 lumber
- 2½ and 3" deck screws
- Galvanized metal stucco lath
- Silicone caulk
- Vegetable oil or other release agent
- Countertop concrete mix or Quikrete® 5000
- Base coat stucco
- Finish coat stucco

Construction Details

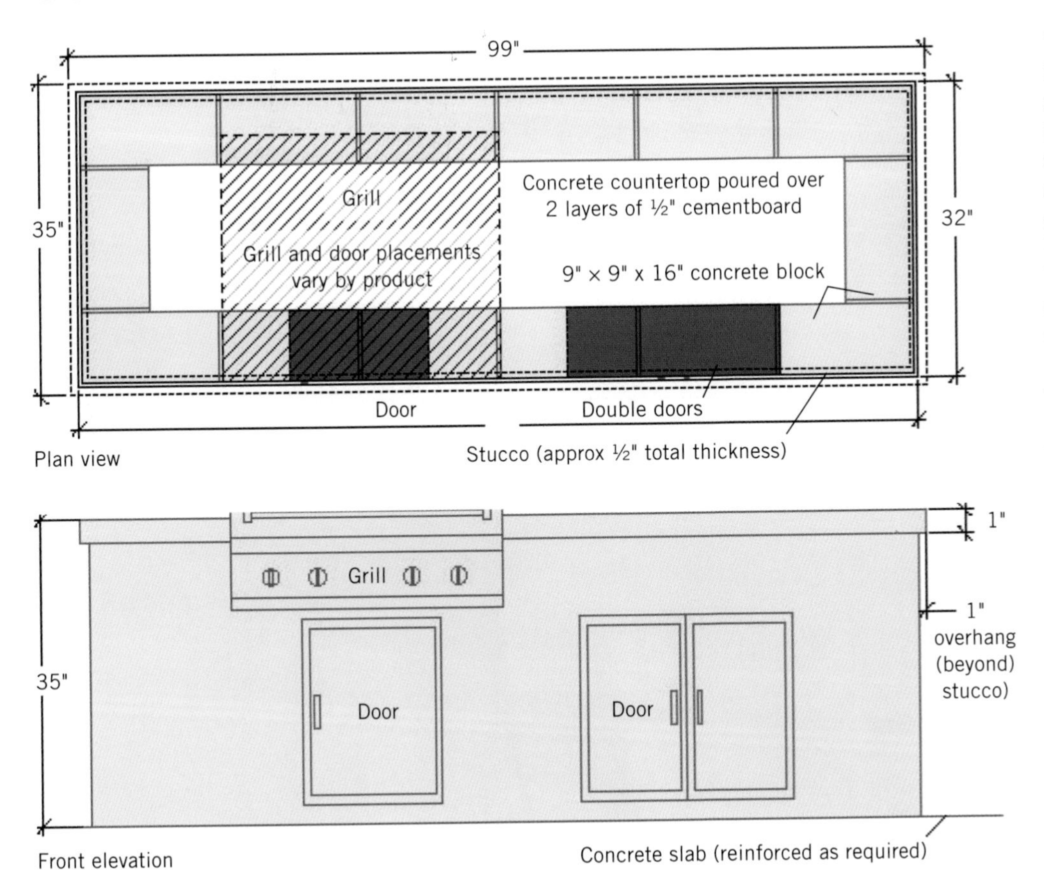

The basic structure of this kitchen consists of five courses of standard 8" × 8" × 16" concrete block. Two mortared layers of ½" cementboard serve as a base for the countertop. The 2"-thick poured concrete layer of the countertop extends 1½" beyond the rough block walls and covers the cementboard edges. The two-coat stucco finish can be tinted during the mixing or painted after it cures. Cabinet doors provide access to storage space inside and to any utility connections for the grill. The kitchen's dimensions can easily be adjusted to accommodate a specific location, cooking equipment, or doors and additional amenities.

PLANNING A KITCHEN PROJECT

Whether you model your project after the one shown here or create your own design, there are a few critical factors to address as part of your initial planning:

- **Foundation** Check with your local building department about foundation requirements for your kitchen. Depending on the kitchen's size and location, you may be allowed to build on top of a standard 4"-thick reinforced concrete patio slab, or you might need frost footings or a reinforced "floating footing" similar to the one shown on page 102 (**Brick Barbecue**).
- **Grill & Door Units** You'll need the exact dimensions of the grill, doors, and any other built-in features before you start building. When shopping for equipment, keep in mind its utility requirements and the type of support system needed for the grill and other large units. Some grills are drop-in and are supported only by the countertop; others must be supported below with a noncombustible, load-bearing material such as concrete block or a poured concrete platform.
- **Utility Hookups** Grills fueled by natural gas require a plumbed gas line, and those with electric starters need an outdoor electrical circuit, both running into the kitchen cabinet. To include a kitchen sink, you'll need a dedicated water line and a drain connection. Outdoor utilities are strictly governed by building codes, so check with the building department for requirements. Generally, the rough-in work for utilities is best left to professionals.

A grill gas line typically extends up into the cabinet space under the grill and is fitted with a shutoff valve.

How to Build the Outdoor Kitchen

Pour the foundation or prepare the slab for the wall construction. To prepare an existing slab, clean the surface thoroughly to remove all dirt, oils, concrete sealers, and paint that could prevent a good bond with mortar.

Dry-lay the first course of block on the foundation to test the layout. If desired, use 2- or 4"-thick solid blocks under the door openings. Snap chalk lines to guide the block installation, and mark the exact locations of the door openings.

Set the first course of block into mortar, following the basic techniques shown on pages 104–105. Cut blocks as needed for the door openings. Lay the second course, offsetting the joints with the first course in a running bond pattern.

Continue laying up the wall, adding reinforcing wire or rebar if required by local building code. Instead of tooling the mortar joints for a concave profile, use a trowel to slice excess mortar from the blocks. This creates a flat surface that's easier to cover with stucco.

Install steel angle lintels to span over the door openings. If an opening is in line with a course of block, mortar the lintels in place on top of the block. Otherwise, use a circular saw with a masonry blade to cut channels for the horizontal leg of the angle. Lintels should span 6" beyond each side of an opening. Slip the lintel into the channels, and then fill the block cells containing the lintel with mortar to secure the lintel in place. Lay a bed of mortar on top of the lintels, then set block into the mortar. Complete the final course of block in the cabinet and let the mortar cure.

Cut two 8-ft.-long sheets of cementboard to match the outer dimensions of the block cabinet. Apply mortar to the tops of the cabinet blocks and then set one layer of cementboard into the mortar. If you will be installing a built-in grill or other accessories, make cutouts in the cementboard with a utility knife or a jigsaw with a remodeler's blade.

Cut pieces to fit for a second layer of cementboard. Apply a bed of mortar to the top of the first panel, and then lay the second layer pieces on top, pressing them into the mortar so the surfaces are level. Let the mortar cure.

(continued)

To create a 1½" overhang for the countertop, build a perimeter band of 2 × 4 lumber; this will serve as the base of the concrete form. Cut the pieces to fit tightly around the cabinet along the top. Fasten the pieces together at their ends with 3" screws so their top edges are flush with the bottom of the cementboard.

Cut vertical 2 × 4 supports to fit snugly between the foundation and the bottom of the 2 × 4 band. Install a support at the ends of each wall and evenly spaced in between. Secure each support with angled screws driven into the band boards.

Build the sides of the countertop form with 2 × 6s cut to fit around the 2 × 4 band. Position the 2 × 6s so their top edges are 2" above the cementboard, and fasten them to the band with 2½" screws.

Form the opening for the grill using 2 × 6 side pieces (no overhang inside opening). Support the edges of the cementboard along the grill cutout with cleats attached to the 2 × 6s. Add vertical supports as needed under the cutout to keep the form from shifting under the weight of the concrete.

Cut a sheet of stucco lath to fit into the countertop form, leaving a 2" space along the inside perimeter of the form. Remove the lath and set it aside. Seal the form joints with a fine bead of silicone caulk and smooth with a finger. After the caulk dries, coat the form boards (not the cementboard) with vegetable oil or other release agent.

Dampen the cementboard with a mist of water. Mix a batch of countertop mix, adding color if desired (see page 118). Working quickly, fill along the edges of the form with concrete, carefully packing it down into the overhang portion by hand.

Fill the rest of the form halfway up with an even layer of concrete. Lay the stucco lath on top; then press it lightly into the concrete with a float. Add the remaining concrete so it's flush with the tops of the 2 × 6s.

Tap along the outsides of the form with a hammer to remove air bubbles trapped against the inside edges. Screed the top of the concrete with a straight 2 × 4 riding along the form sides. Add concrete as needed to fill in low spots so the surface is perfectly flat. *(continued)*

After the bleed water disappears, float the concrete with a wood or magnesium float. The floated surface should be flat and smooth but will still have a somewhat rough texture. Be careful not to overfloat and draw water to the surface.

A few hours after floating, finish the countertop as desired. A few passes with a steel finishing trowel yields the smoothest surface. Hold the leading edge of the trowel up and work in circular strokes. Let the concrete set for a while between passes.

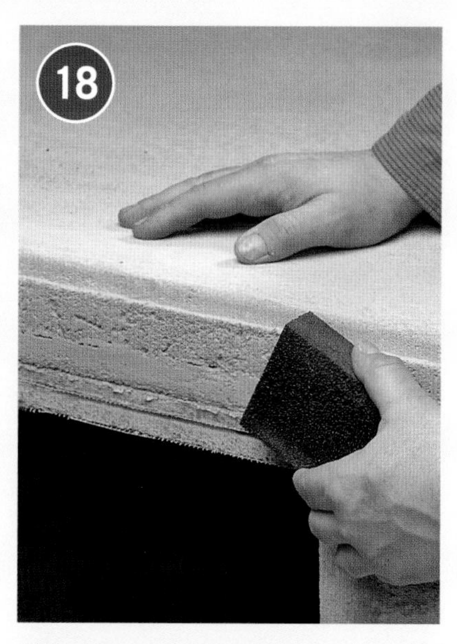

Moist-cure the countertop with a fine water mist for three to five days. Remove the form boards. If desired, smooth the countertop edges with an abrasive brick and/or a diamond pad or sandpaper. After the concrete cures, apply a food-safe sealer to help prevent staining.

Prepare for door installation in the cabinet. Outdoor cabinet doors are usually made of stainless steel, and typically are installed by hanging hinges or flanges with masonry anchors. Drill holes for masonry anchors in the concrete block, following the door manufacturer's instructions.

TIP

Honeycombs or air voids can be filled using a cement slurry of cement and water applied with a rubber float. If liquid cement color was used in your countertop concrete mix, color should be added to the wet cement paste. Some experimentation will be necessary.

Finish installing and hanging the doors. Test the door operations and make sure to caulk around the edges with high-quality silicone caulk.

NOTE: Doors shown here are best installed before the stucco finish is applied to the cabinet. Other doors may be easier to install following a different sequence.

To finish the cabinet walls, begin by dampening the contrete block and then applying a ⅜"-thick base coat of stucco, following the steps on page 79. Apply an even layer over the walls; then smooth the surface with a wood float and moist-cure the stucco for 48 hours or as directed by the manufacturer.

Apply a finish coat of tinted stucco that's at least ⅛" thick. Evenly saturate the base coat stucco surface with water prior to applying the the finish coat. Texture the surface as desired. Moist-cure the stucco for several days as directed.

Set the grill into place, make the gas connection, then check it carefully for leaks. Permanently install the grill following the manufacturer's directions. The joints around grills are highly susceptible to water intrusion; seal them thoroughly with an approved caulk to help keep moisture out of the cabinet space below.

Patio Prep Cart

TOOLS & MATERIALS

- 1 × 4" × 8' cedar boards (18)
- 2 × 4" × 8' cedar boards (4)
- ¾" × 4 × 8' cedar plywood (1)
- ½ × 3" × 5' cementboard (1)
- ¾ × 24" × 48' exterior plywood (1)
- 12 × 12" floor tiles (8)
- Exterior-rated screws (1¼", 2½")
- Lag screws (16 @ ¼" × 1½")
- 3" utility hinges (2)
- Casters (4)
- Door handle (1)
- Catch (1)

This elegant rolling cook's cart will take your outdoor cooking to a higher level without breaking your bank account. Whether the point is to impress or simply to make your outdoor entertaining a bit more pleasant, setting up an outdoor kitchen that revolves around this clever cart and an ordinary grill is easy. And, because this cart (and most grills) are on wheels, they're easy to move as needed and to roll away into storage.

This cart features 8 square feet of countertop space, a storage cabinet with shelves, and a dedicated place for a refrigerator. The sides are made from 1 × 4 cedar or a similar exterior-grade lumber. Use corrosion-resistant screws to assemble this cart. The screws that attach the siding are driven from the outside, leaving the heads exposed to act as a design feature.

This outdoor kitchen cart employs eight 12 × 12-inch tiles for the countertop, minimizing the joints in the countertop surface. To simplify construction, the tiles are set with construction adhesive (instead of thinset mortar) and the joints between the tiles are filled with exterior caulk (instead of tile grout).

Both attractive and functional, this rolling cook's cart with space for a refrigerator will make your deck or patio almost as convenient as your kitchen for entertaining friends and family.

PATIO PREP CART

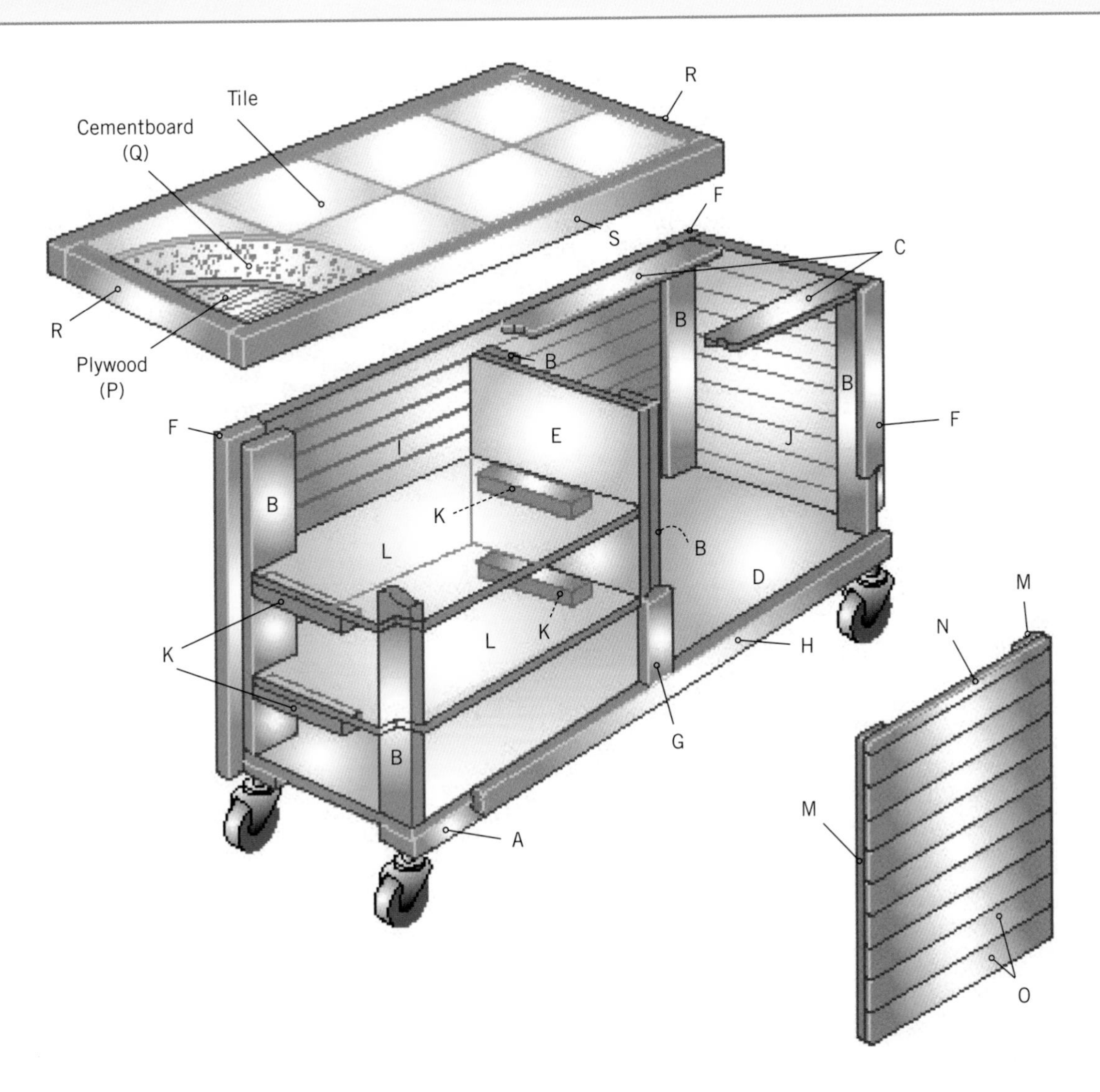

CUTTING LIST

KEY	PART	DIMENSION	PCS.	MATERIAL
A	Bottom supports	1½ × 3½ × 46"	2	Cedar
B	Posts	1½ × 3½ × 35"	6	Cedar
C	Top rails	⅞ × 3½ × 46"	2	Cedar
D	Bottom panel	¾ × 22 × 46"	1	Cedar plywood
E	Center panel	¾ × 22 × 35"	1	Cedar plywood
F	Corner stiles	⅞ × 2½ × 37¼"	4	Cedar
G	Front center stile	⅞ × 2½ × 35⅜"	1	Cedar
H	Front bottom rail	¾ × 1¾ × 42¾"	1	Cedar
I	Back siding	⅞ × 3½ × 42¼"	10	Cedar
J	Side siding	⅞ × 3½ × 22"	20	Cedar

KEY	PART	DIMENSION	PCS.	MATERIAL
K	Shelf supports	⅞ × 1 × 17"	4	Cedar
L	Shelves	¾ × 19½ × 21¾"	2	Cedar plywood
M	Door stiles	⅞ × 3½ × 34½"	2	Cedar
N	Top door siding	⅞ × 1 × 18½"	1	Cedar
O	Door siding	⅞ × 3½ × 18½"	9	Cedar
P	Worksurface subbase	¾ × 24 × 48"	1	Ext. plywood
Q	Tile backer	½ × 24 × 48"	1	Cementboard
R	Side edging	⅞ × 1½ × 24"	2	Cedar
S	Front/back edging	⅞ × 1½ × 49½"	2	Cedar

How to Build the Patio Prep Cart

Build the Frame

This outdoor kitchen cart is essentially a skeleton of 2 × 4 cedar wrapped in cedar siding and capped off with large tiles. Start by building the skeleton: that is, the frame. Cut the bottom supports, posts, and top rails to length. Cut the bottom panel and center panel to length and width. Attach two of the posts to the center panel with 1¼" screws. Place the center panel and bottom panel on their sides and attach the bottom panel to the posts with 2½" screws (photo 1). With the panels on their edges, attach two of the corner posts to the bottom panel. Flip the assembly right-side up and attach one of the top rails to the top of the corner posts and center panel post. Attach the other two corner posts and top rail (photo 2). Attach the bottom supports to the bottom panel with 1¼" screws.

Install the Corners, Trim & Siding

Cut the corner stiles to length and width. Attach the corner stiles to the corner posts with four 1¼" screws. Drill a countersunk, ⅛"-diameter pilot hole for each screw (photo 3). Cut the front-bottom rail to length and width and attach it to the front-bottom support with four 1¼" screws and decorative finish washers. Cut the side siding and back siding pieces to length. Drill two countersunk pilot holes in each end of each siding board. Space the holes 1" in from the ends and ¾" in from the edges. Attach the siding boards to the corner posts with 1¼" screws, spacing the boards ¼" apart (photo 4). Drill a 1¼"-diameter hole near the bottom of the back of the refrigerator section for the power cord to fit through.

Install the Shelves

The shelves for this outdoor cart are optional. As shown, they're spaced to allow storage of items of varying height, such as plates and cups. But if you want to store taller items, such as bags of charcoal or a turkey fryer, eliminate the shelves from the plan.

Measure and mark the shelf heights on the inside faces of the left side siding and center divider. Here, the shelves are spaced so the lowest shelf opening is

Attach the bottom panel to the posts. Drive 2½" screws through the underside of the bottom panel and into the ends of the center panel posts.

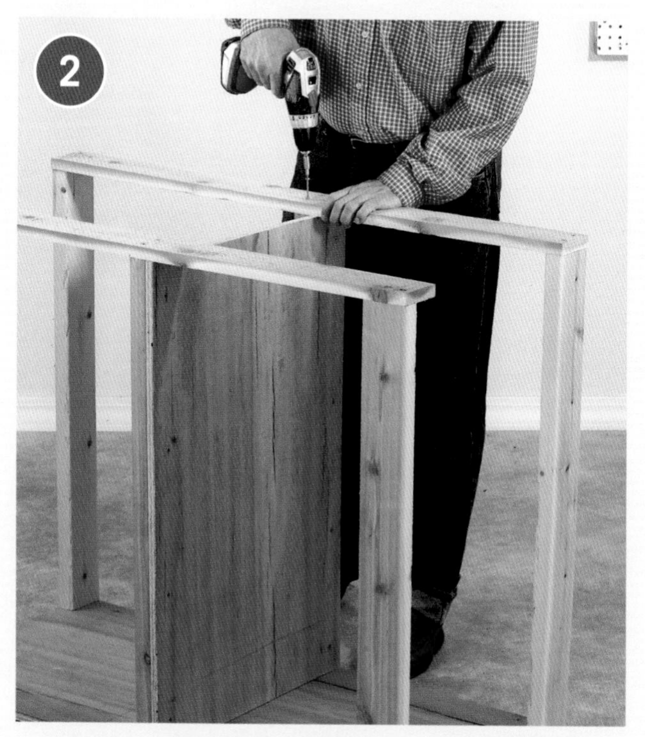

Install corner posts and top rails. Each top rail should be attached to a corner post and a center panel post with 2½" screws. Drive one screw into each post.

Install cornerboards. Attach the corner stiles to the corner posts with 1¼" screws. Align the inside edges of the stiles and posts.

Add siding. Drill two countersunk pilot holes through each end of each siding board. Locate the holes 1" from the ends and ¾" from the top and bottom edges. Attach the siding boards with 1¼" screws, spaced with a ¼" gap between boards.

15" high. The middle opening is 10" high and the top opening is 8" high. The shelf supports are sized so the shelves will not interfere with the front corner posts. Attach the shelf supports with 1¼" screws driven through countersunk pilot holes in the supports and into the cabinet walls. Cut the shelves from ¾"-thick plywood (preferably cedar plywood). Cut 1½ × 3½" notches in the left corners of each shelf board to fit around the posts. Drive a few brads down through the shelves and into the supports to secure them (photo 5).

Build the Door

Cut the door stiles to length. Cut the door siding to length and the top door siding board to length and width. Drill two countersunk pilot holes in each end of each full-width door siding board. Space the holes 1" in from the ends and ¾" in from the edges. Drill one countersunk pilot hole in each end of the top door siding board. Attach the siding boards to the door stiles with 1¼" screws (photo 6).

Attach the Wheels & Hardware

Tip the cabinet upside down and place one caster in each corner (here, 2½" casters are being installed).

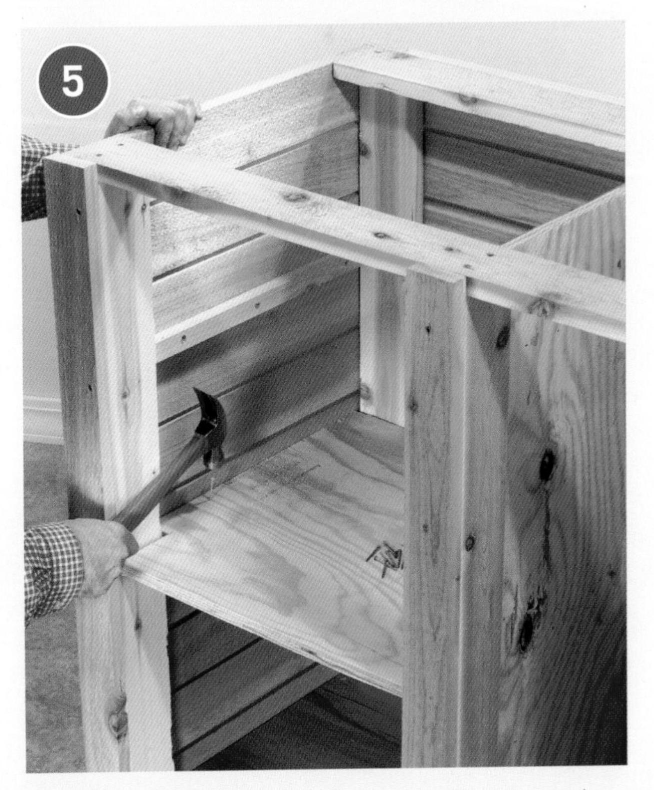

Install the shelves. Attach the shelf supports with screws and then tack the shelves into position with 1¼" brads. *(continued)*

Attach the door siding boards to the door stiles. The top door siding board is attached with only one screw in each end.

Attach the casters. Position each caster and drill pilot holes for each caster screw. Attach the casters with 1/4 × 1 1/4" lag screws.

Mark the caster screw holes and drill 3/16" pilot holes for each screw. Fasten the casters with 1/4 × 1 1/2" hot-dipped lag screws (photo 7). To hang the door, attach zinc-plated or brass hinges (a pair of 3" butt hinges will do) to the door and the left corner post and corner stile (photo 8). Also add a handle (an aluminum door pull installed vertically is used here) as well as a latch and strikeplate to hold the door closed.

Build & Attach the Top

The top for this cart features a 3/4"-thick plywood subbase that supports a cementboard backer for the tiles (here, eight 12 × 12" porcelain tiles). Cut the plywood subbase to size from exterior plywood and attach it to the top rails with 1 1/4" deck screws. Cut a piece of tile backer board (here, 1/2"-thick cementboard) to 24 × 48". Attach the backer board to the subbase with construction adhesive and 1" screws (make sure the screwheads are recessed below the cementboard surface). Attach the tiles to the backer board with construction adhesive (photo 9).

Cut the top sides, front, and back edging pieces to length from cedar 1 × 2. Drill countersunk, 1/8"-diameter pilot holes in the edging pieces and attach them to the subbase edges with construction adhesive and brads (photo 10). Fill gaps around tile with caulk. Apply a clear, UV-protectant finish to the wood surface and seal the tiles.

Hang the door and install hardware. Fasten the door hinges to the door (or doors if you choose to cover each opening) and then attach the door to the cart frame. Use a 1/4" spacer under the door to position it.

Install the tile work surface. Instead of traditional thinset mortar, exterior construction adhesive is being used because it better withstands temperature and humidity changes.

Attach countertop edging. Made from strips of 1 × 2 cedar, the edging hides the countertop edges and protects the tile. Fill the gaps around the edge tiles and between tiles with caulk.

Pitmaster's Locker

Supplies and accessories for your outdoor grilling and barbecuing have special storage requirements. Some, such as charcoal starter fluid and propane tanks and bottles, are hazardous, flammable chemicals that should be locked safely away outside of the house or garage. Other supplies, such as big bags of charcoal briquettes, turkey fryers, or starter chimneys, are bulky and often dirty or dusty. Additional tools, like grill brushes, thermometers, rib racks, and Texas-size kitchen utensils, are best kept together in a neat area close to your grill. This Pitmaster's Locker addresses all of these concerns in a rugged-looking package that fits in well with today's popular grilling equipment.

The frame for this grill locker is made with solid aluminum angle iron, sold at most building centers. Aluminum is rigid, sturdy, and withstands exposure to the elements very well. It is also relatively easy to drill, which you will appreciate. Because the metals market is fairly volatile, costs for aluminum can run on the high side. But if you buy in volume, you can usually save a little money. Our eight pieces of 72-inch aluminum angle cost us $130 from an Internet seller (this is at a time of high metal costs). If you like this design but want to save some money, you can substitute paintable hardwood, such as poplar, for the frame parts. This requires recalculating the shelf and panel dimensions, however.

The lower shelf of this locker has 24 inches of height capacity. If you plan to store a 20-pound propane tank on this shelf, you can lower the supports for the middle shelf by 6 inches and still have enough room for the 17½-inch-tall standard tanks. This creates a middle shelf that has 30 inches of height capacity (or two shorter shelves).

For the serious grill cook (a Pitmaster in barbecuer's parlance), a lockable, dedicated storage locker is the best place to keep tools, fuel, and other supplies organized and safe.

TOOLS & MATERIALS

- 1⁄16 × 1½ × 72" solid aluminum angle (8)
- ⅜" × 4 × 8' sheet rough cedar siding (2)
- ¾" × 4 × 8' exterior plywood (1)
- ¼ × ¾" × 8' wood shelf edge (1)
- 1 × 2" × 8' cedar boards (2)
- Exterior hasp with padlock
- 2 × 2" butt hinges (3)
- ¼ × ¾" bolts
- ¼" lock nuts
- ¾" hex-head wood screws
- Aluminum pop rivets

PITMASTER'S LOCKER

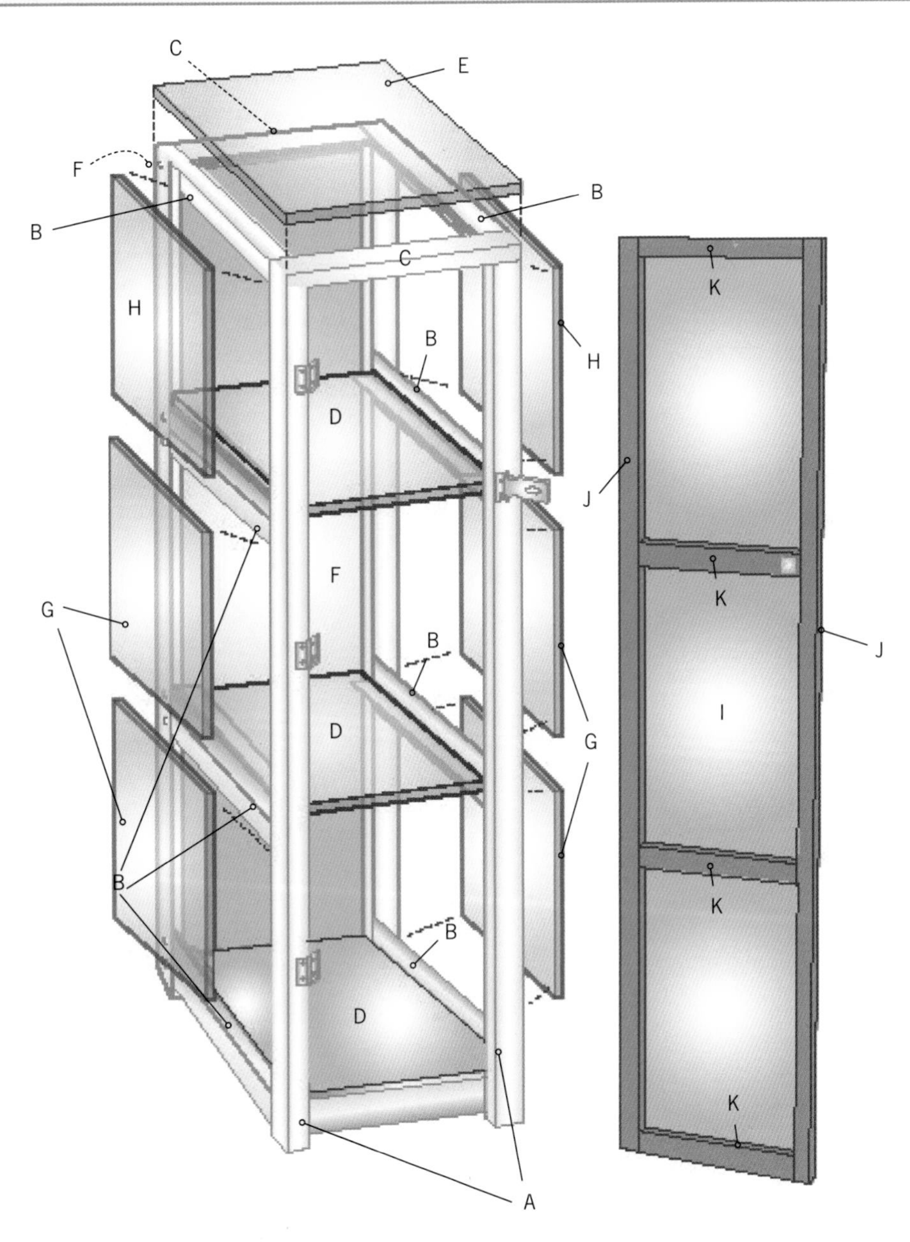

CUTTING LIST

KEY	PART	DIMENSION	PCS.	MATERIAL
A	Frame legs	1⁄16 × 1½ × 72"	4	Aluminum angle
B	Shelf supports	1⁄16 × 1½ × 18"	12	Aluminum angle
C	Frame tops	1⁄16 × 1½ × 18¼"	2	Aluminum angle
D	Shelves	¾ × 17 × 16"	3	Ext. plywood
E	Top*	¾ × 17½ × 18½"	1	Ext. plywood
F	Back panel	⅜ × 18 × 70"	1	Cedar siding
G	Side panels	⅜ × 16 × 23½"	4	Cedar siding
H	Side panels (top)	⅜ × 16 × 21"	2	Cedar siding
I	Door panel	⅜ × 14 × 67"	1	Ext. plywood
J	Door stiles	¾ × 1½ × 68"	2	Cedar
K	Door rails	¾ × 1½ × 12"	4	Cedar
L	Top trim (opt.)**	1 × 1" × cut to fit	4	Corner molding

*Exposed edges finished with ¼ × ¾" wood shelf edge

**Not shown

How to Build the Pitmaster's Locker

Make the Metal Frame

The framework for this locker is built from solid aluminum angle (1/16" thick × 1½" wide each direction). Although aluminum is very rigid, it is also relatively soft and very workable for cutting and drilling. You can easily cut the metal parts for this project with a hacksaw, though keeping the cuts straight can be tricky. If you have access to a metal cutoff saw, it will save a lot of time—you might consider renting one. Do not install an abrasive blade in a power miter saw. You can also use a reciprocating saw or a jigsaw with a bimetal blade, as seen here (photo 1). Whichever saw you use, clean up and deburr the cut edges with a bench grinder.

Lay out shelf locations on the frame legs with a wax crayon or pencil (avoid permanent markers, as they work but the marks cannot be erased). Install shelf supports between pairs of legs at selected heights. Clamp each support to each leg with a locking pliers. Drill one ¼" guide hole in the middle of each joint (photo 2). Use a carbide-tipped twist bit.

Cut the aluminum angle for the frame parts (top) and then deburr the cut ends on a bench grinder (lower). Don't overdo it on the grinder or use a file.

Drill guide holes for bolts. Clamp the part for each joint together with locking pliers and then drill for one ¼" bolt per joint.

Assemble the frame. Secure each frame joint with a ¼ × ¾" bolt and lock nut. If you're able to locate aluminum fasteners, use them; otherwise use stainless-steel or hot-dipped fasteners.

TIP: Lubricate the drilling point with a drop of cutting oil before drilling. Add more oil if the metal begins to smoke. Once the guide hole is drilled, insert a ¼ × ¾" bolt and add a locknut on the interior side (photo 3). Hand-tighten the nut, but wait until the entire frame is assembled and squared before tightening nuts all the way.

After all of the joints are secured with hand-tightened bolts, check the assembly with a framing square and adjust as needed. Begin fully tightening the locknuts. Grasp each nut with a locking pliers and tighten the bolt head with a socket and ratchet or cordless impact driver (photo 4).

Add the Plywood Panels & Shelves

Cut the shelves to size from ¾"-thick plywood (use quality plywood such as AB or BC as opposed to sheathing or CDX). *(continued)*

Assemble the frame by tightening the locknuts onto the bolts. Hand-tighten all nuts first and then check the frame to make sure it is square. Tighten the nuts with a cordless impact driver or a ratcheting socket set.

Attach the panels using aluminum pop rivets driven through guide holes in the frame and the panels.

Cut the panels from rough-textured cedar siding panels (these come in 4 × 8' sheets, usually around ⅜" thick). Sand and stain both faces and the edges of the panels and shelves with exterior stain before installing them.

Attach the back panel, top panel, and side panels in the correct locations with ¾" pop rivets (photo 5). Clamp each panel in place and drill guide holes for the rivets through the frames and the panels. Install the pop rivets from the exterior side of the cabinet.

Hang the door. Attach the hinges to the metal frame first and then attach the other plates to the back of the door on the edge with no shelf edge molding.

Install the back panel first because it helps to square up the cabinet.

Hang the Door & Install Hardware

The locker door is sized to fit in between the metal frame members, and it closes against the slightly recessed shelf edges. It is made from ⅜"-thick siding and framed with 1 × 2 trim. Install three butt hinges to the left leg with bolts and lock nuts. You will probably need to enlarge the screw holes in the hinge plates to accept the ¼"-diameter bolts. After installing all three butt hinges, attach the edge of the door to the free hinge plates (photo 6). Test the door. If it works properly, attach the locking hasp. Use exterior-rated wood glue and 1" brass brads to attach ¼"-thick × ¾"-wide wood shelf edge to the front edges of the shelves (photo 7).

Make the panels and shelves. Cut the shelves and door to size from exterior plywood and attach wood shelf edge molding to select edges as instructed. Cut the side, back, and top panels from cedar plywood (siding). Stain the parts before installing them in the frame.

Outdoor Kitchen Walls & Countertops

Loaded with convenient work surfaces and a dedicated grill space, the outdoor kitchen has changed backyard grilling forever. This roomy kitchen can be the perfect addition to any patio or garden retreat. It's made entirely of concrete blocks and not only looks great, it's also incredibly easy to build.

The design of this kitchen comes from a manufacturer (see Resources, page 172) that supplies all of the necessary masonry materials on two pallets. As shown, the project's footprint is about 98 × 109 inches and includes a 58-inch-wide space for setting in a grill. Square columns can provide work surfaces on either side of the grill, so you'll want to keep them conveniently close, but if you need a little more or a little less room for your grill, you can simply adjust the number of blocks that go into the front wall section enclosing the grill alcove.

Opposite the grill station is a 32-inch-tall countertop capped with large square pavers, or patio stones, for a finished look. This countertop has a lower surface for food prep and a higher surface for serving or dining. A low side wall connects the countertop with the grill area and adds just the right amount of enclosure to complete the kitchen space.

TOOLS & MATERIALS

- Masonry outdoor kitchen kit (concrete wall block, concrete patio stones)
- Chalk line
- Framing square
- Straight board
- Level
- Caulk gun
- Exterior-grade concrete adhesive
- Tape measure
- Eye and ear protection
- Work gloves

This all-masonry outdoor kitchen comes ready to assemble on any solid patio surface, or you can build it over a prepared gravel base anywhere in your landscape (check with the manufacturer for base requirements). For a custom design, similar materials are available to purchase separately and the installation would be more or less the same as shown here. Discuss the project with the manufacturer for specifics. If you decide to build just a part of this kitchen (the bar, for example), review the setup and site prep steps at the beginning of this project.

How to Build the Outdoor Kitchen

Dry-lay the project on the installation surface. This overview of the first course of blocks shows how the kitchen is constructed with five columns and two wall sections. Laying out the first course carefully and making sure the wall sections are square ensures the rest of the project will go smoothly.

Create squared reference lines for the kitchen walls after you remove the dry-laid blocks. Snap a chalk line representing the outside face of the front wall. Mark the point where the side wall will meet the front wall. Place a framing square at the mark and trace a perpendicular line along the leg of the square. Snap a chalk line along the pencil line to represent the side wall, or use the edge of a patio as this boundary (as shown). To confirm that the lines are square, mark the front-wall line 36" from the corner and the side-wall line 48" from the corner. The distance between the marks should be 60". If not, re-snap one of the chalk lines until the measurements work out.

(continued)

Begin laying the first course of block. Starting in the 90° corner of the chalk lines, set four blocks at right angles to begin the corner column. Make sure all blocks are placed together tightly. Set the long wall with blocks laid end to end, followed by another column.

Finish laying the first course, including two more columns, starting at the side wall. Use a straight board as a guide to make sure the columns form a straight line. To check for square, measure between the long wall and the short wall at both ends; the measurements should be equal. Adjust the short-wall columns as needed.

Set the second course. Add the second course of blocks to each of the columns, rotating the pattern 90° to the first course. Set the blocks for the long and side walls, leaving about a 2" gap in between the corner column and the first block. Set the remaining wall blocks with the same gap so the blocks overlap the joints in the first course.

Set the third course. Lay the third-course blocks using the same pattern as in the first course. For appearance and stability, make sure the faces of the blocks are flush with one another and that the walls and columns are plumb. Use a level to align the blocks and check for plumb.

Install the remaining courses. The higher courses of wall block are glued in place. Set the courses in alternating patterns, as before, gluing each block in place with concrete adhesive.

Build the short wall overhang. Starting at one end of the short wall, glue wall blocks along the tops of the columns with concrete adhesive. Position blocks perpendicular to the length of the short wall, overhanging the columns by 3".

Complete the short wall top. Create the counter surface for the short wall by gluing patio stones to the tops of the columns and overhanging blocks. Position the stones for the lower surface against the ends of the overhanging blocks. Position the upper-surface stones so they extend beyond the overhanging blocks slightly on the outside ends and a little more so on the inside ends.

Cap the corner columns. Finish the two corner columns with wall blocks running parallel to the side wall. Glue the cap pieces in place on the columns using concrete adhesive. Make sure the blocks are fitted tightly together.

TAILGATING

Tailgating Gear

Sports and cookout food are natural companions. And no more so than before a big game, when fans of all kinds gather in parking lots to fill up on tasty grub before watching their favorite team in action. Tailgating has become so common and popular that the game itself may take a back seat to the parking-lot spread a good grill cook whips up.

But if you're really going to satisfy the appetites of friends and fellow fans, a portable hibachi won't cut it. You need a real-world grill that you can bring along with you, one that has the capacity to cook everything you want to cook, easy and quickly.

The best tailgating gear can either be towed behind or is designed to sit comfortably in the bed of a pickup. But in either case, the gear has to work every bit as well as a high-quality backyard setup. The **Tailgate Smoker** on page 140 fills the bill, providing plenty of room for your favorite tailgate dishes, and a convenient design that helps you maintain optimal smoking temperatures. Because equipment and accessories are every bit as important as the cooker for a tailgate cookout, you'll find a **Tailgating Toolbox Grill** on page 146. And you'll need something to wash down all that great food, so why not make the **Pub Table Cooler** on page 164?

The beauty of these projects is that they are all fairly adaptable, so that you can use them with the vehicle you own—whether you're sporting a three-quarter-ton pickup truck, or a rolling to the game in a trusty motorhome. The focus remains on efficient cooking that will create the best cookout food possible. Even if you do end up wolfing it down in a parking lot.

Tailgate Smoker

Grilling has always been the standard way to cook for tailgating, but if you're set up early enough, why not do a little smoking? Better yet, why not have the option of grilling *or* smoking? This handy little cooker gives you just that, and you can easily build it during a single preseason game.

The Tailgate Smoker starts out as a portable-size kettle grill. To turn it into a smoker, all you have to add is a large aluminum cooking pot with a few modifications, plus a pizza pan or pie plate to serve as a heat deflector. You don't have to make any changes to the kettle grill, so it works like it always has with the smoker pot removed. The pot simply rests on top of the kettle base, the kettle's original grill fits right inside the pot, and the kettle lid caps it all off. You'll spend less time setting up your smoker than you will choosing your next beverage.

The small size and upright-barrel design of this smoker make it incredibly fuel-efficient. It's ideal for hot smoking (see **Smoking Temperatures: Cold, Warm, and Hot** on page 25) or burning charcoal and wood chips or chunks in the kettle base. It's also good for warm smoking or short-term cold smoking, using just a cold smoker for heat and smoke (see **Cold Smokers** on page 28).

The trick to making this project as easy as it looks is finding the right pot for your grill. In general, a 32-quart aluminum steamer pot is the right size for a 14-inch kettle grill, but sizes for both pots and grills vary among brands and models. Follow the actual dimensions of your grill: the *inside* diameter of the kettle base should be just a hair smaller than the *outside* diameter of the pot. The grill grate must fit inside the pot, but it doesn't have to be a perfect fit because the grate rests on bolts, and a little wiggle room is helpful for lifting out the grate. You can buy steamer pots online or at local restaurant supply stores. If you shop locally, you can bring your kettle grill with you for a test-fit.

TOOLS & MATERIALS

- Safety glasses
- Standard tape measure
- Cloth tape measure
- Drill-driver
- ¼" drill bit
- Step drill bit (must drill up to 1" diameter) or 1" hole saw
- Open end or adjustable wrenches
- Screwdriver
- Eye and ear protection
- Work gloves
- 14" kettle-type portable grill (1)
- 32-quart aluminum pot (steamer pot) (1)
- 12" aluminum pie pan or pizza pan (1)
- ¼ × 1" stainless-steel bolts with washers and nuts (3)
- ¼ × 3" stainless-steel round-head stove bolts with washers and nuts (3)
- High-temp spray paint (stove paint; optional)
- Painter's tape (optional)
- Plastic bag or newspaper (optional)
- Barbecue thermometer (with mounting threads and nut)

WOOD
CHIPS

TAILGATE SMOKER

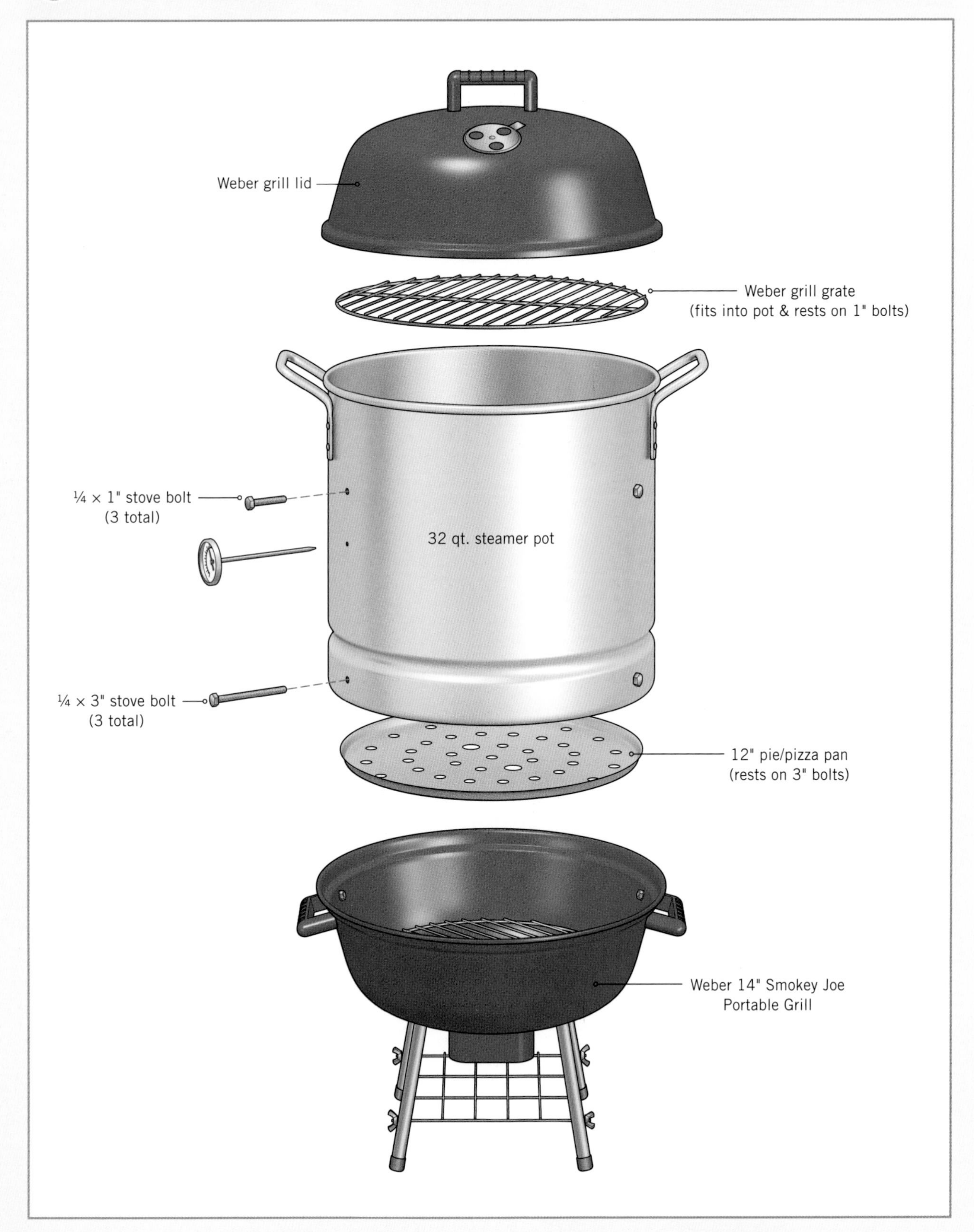

How to Build the Tailgate Smoker

Measure straight down 4½" from the top edge of the pot and make a mark with a pencil. Do the same thing at a few more places around the outside of the pot, at roughly equal intervals. The spacing is not critical.

Wrap a cloth tape measure around the pot so its top edge is aligned with the 4½" marks. Note the total measurement of the pot circumference, and divide this number into thirds. For example, if the pot measures 46", dividing by 3 gives you 15⅓", or about 15⅜". Make three marks that are 15⅜" apart, marking along the top edge of the tape measure; this is where you will drill for the grill supports.

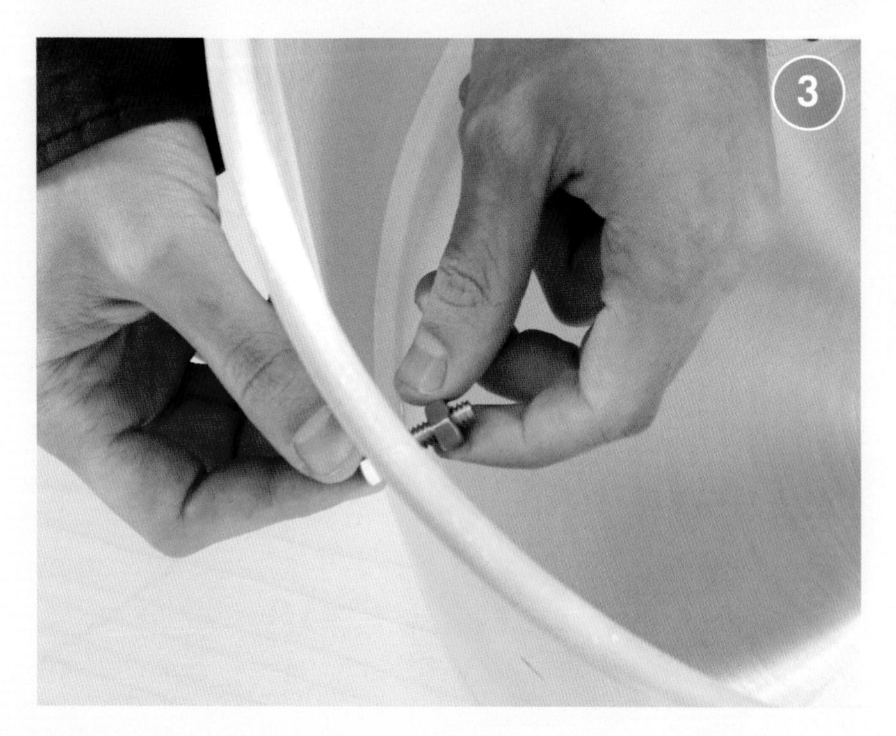

Drill a ¼" hole through the side of the pot at each of the three marks, drilling from the outside. Insert a ¼ × 1" stove bolt through each hole so the bolt head is on the outside. Secure the bolt with a washer and nut on the inside of the pot, tightening the nut with a screwdriver and wrench.

WARNING: Always wear eye protection when drilling metal.

(continued)

Repeat the same process to install three evenly spaced bolts, just below the ring near the bottom of the pot, or about 1⅜" above the bottom of the pot. Use ¼ × 3" stove bolts, with a washer and nut on the inside of the pot, as with the grill support bolts.

Set the pot upside down onto an old towel on the floor. Drill 1" holes through the bottom of the pot, using a step bit or a 1" hole saw. Drill about 22 to 25 holes, spacing them approximately evenly, and keeping the outermost holes about ¾" from the outer edge of the pot.

Paint the outside of the pot, if desired, using high-temp stove paint or automotive paint (made for car engine parts). Mask off any parts you don't want to paint, such as the handles and the pot rim, with painter's tape. Cover the pot interior with a plastic bag or newspaper.

TIP: A smoker for tailgating is perfect for a custom logo, which works really well on the smooth surface of the pot (see **Painting Custom Logos** on page 155). Apply the paint in three or more very thin layers for best results. Let each coat dry as directed.

Drill a ¼" hole for the thermometer through the side of the pot, locating the hole in a convenient location about 6½" below the top rim, or about 2" below the grill grate. Insert the probe end of the thermometer through the hole and secure it on the inside of the pot with the provided mounting nut. Your smoker is ready to use! See **Setting Up the Tailgate Smoker** below.

SETTING UP THE TAILGATE SMOKER

Perfect for hot smoking, the Tailgate Smoker works well with a cooking temperature between 220° and 250°F. The best fuel source to use is hardwood charcoal, which can burn at a low rate for long periods. You can also add small amounts of wood chips to the coals for extra flavor. Do not use conventional charcoal briquettes, as the unpleasant smoke produced early in the burn can directly flavor the food.

To set up the smoker for cooking, start a load of charcoal in a chimney starter (see page 36), and arrange a load of new charcoal on the coal grate of the kettle grill. When the chimney charcoal is ready, add it to the coals in the kettle. You can also start the fire directly in the kettle.

Place the pie pan or pizza pan onto the lower bolt supports inside the pot. If desired, you can cover the pan with aluminum foil to make it easier to clean. Another option is to place a small bowl of water on top of the pan to add the properties of a water smoker.

Place the grill grate onto the upper set of bolts, then add the food to the grill. Set the pot onto the kettle base, and add the lid. Adjust the dampers on the kettle base and the lid to achieve the desired amount of smoke and maintain the desired temperature.

Tailgating Toolbox Grill

A classic steel toolbox is the perfect thing to turn into a portable grill: it's steel, so it won't burn; it's durable enough to bounce around in the back of a truck; and it has its own locking lid and handle, so it's ready for transport. Not to mention the obvious cool factor. But if you want a tough little grill that performs like a real cooker, there's more to the conversion than emptying out an old toolbox and adding a grill grate. This project covers all the essentials:

- **Choosing a box:** You can use almost any well-built steel toolbox, but be aware of weight and portability. A medium-size box measuring about 8 inches wide × 9 inches tall × 20 inches long is a good place to start. You can go a little bigger as long as the box isn't too heavy. A box designed with a removable tray is handy because you can set the cooking grate on the tray supports, but if you don't have these, you can easily add bolts to support the grate. All of the dimensions given here can be adjusted to fit your box.

- **Stripping the paint:** You must strip all of the original paint from the box, inside and out, because standard paint (even factory-applied paint) can't handle the high heat of the fire. You can repaint the outside of the grill with high-temp stove paint or with an automotive clear-coat (used on engine parts). A new paint job prevents rust and is the perfect opportunity to customize your box (see **Painting Custom Logos** on page 155).

- **Adding ventilation:** Even charcoal doesn't burn well without airflow. Adding a coal grate and ventilation holes helps the fire start quickly and burn more evenly without getting choked with ash.

- **Replacing the handles:** Replace any plastic handle with a custom wood handle (because plastic melts). If your box has metal handles, you might keep the originals, but be aware that they'll get hot, and they're hard to grab when they swivel and rest against the box.

When your toolbox conversion is complete, burn a hot fire inside the grill, with both grates in place, to burn off any residual coatings and to make sure everything works well before using it for cooking.

TOOLS & MATERIALS

Eye and ear protection
Heavy work gloves
Chemical-resistant gloves (for stripping paint)
Paintbrush
Putty knife
Rag
Drill-driver
Grinder or rotary tool with sanding disc (optional)
⅛", ¼", and ½" drill bits
Metal file
Adjustable wrenches (2)
Jigsaw with wood- and metal-cutting blades
Chemical paint stripper
½ × 3" hex bolts (4) with washers and nuts (8)
1¼" round-head stove bolts with washers and nuts (4); add more bolts and nuts (3) and more washers for optional prop stick (4)
Sandpaper
1¼"-diameter × 20"-long hardwood dowel
High-temp spray paint (stove paint)
2 × 4' steel expanded metal sheet (1), 13 gauge, ¾" mesh (plain steel, not galvanized)

TAILGATING TOOLBOX GRILL

CUTTING LIST

KEY	PART	DIMENSIONS	PCS.	MATERIAL
A	Handle	1¼ × 6½"	3	1¼" hardwood dowel
B	Coal grate	Cut to fit	1	Steel expanded metal sheet
C	Cooking grate	Cut to fit	1	Steel expanded metal sheet or grill grate

SIDE VIEW

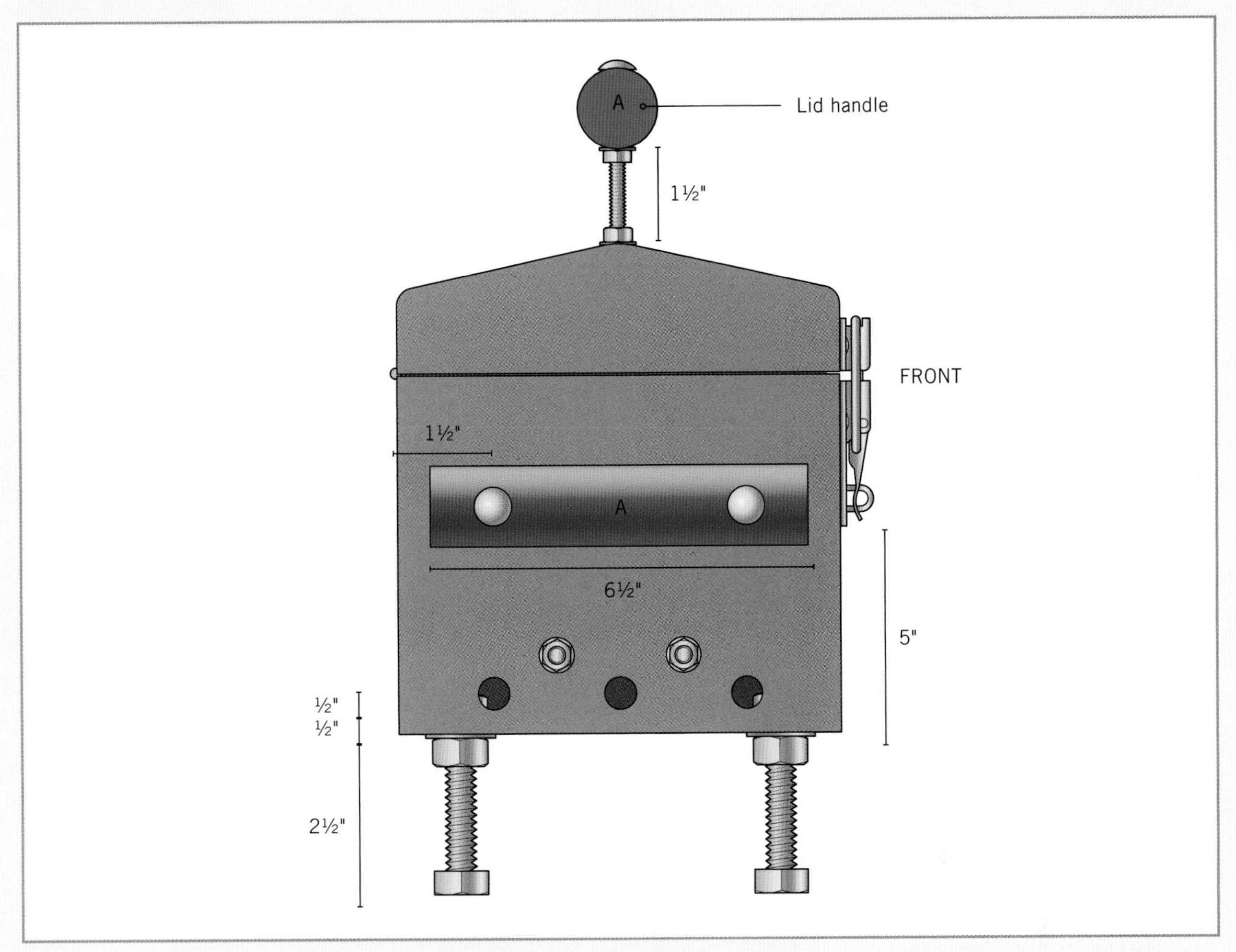

INTERIOR CUTAWAY

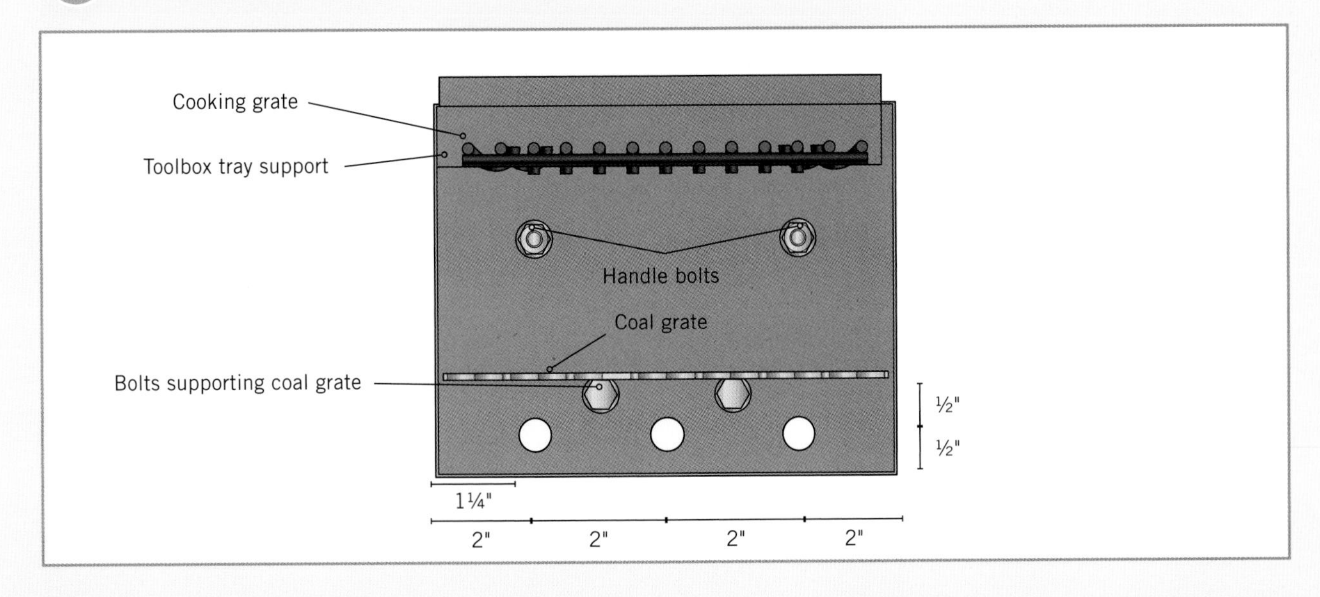

How to Build the Tailgating Toolbox Grill

Prepare the toolbox for paint-stripping by removing the old handle (if desired), the tool tray, and any other removable hardware. If the handle is metal (not plastic), you may opt to keep it, but it will likely get very hot when you're using the grill; be sure to use gloves or hot pads.

Coat the outside or inside surfaces of the box with a gel-type paint remover. Toolboxes have tough factory finishes that require a strong paint stripper. Wear safety glasses and chemical-resistant gloves when applying and removing the stripper. Let the stripper work for the recommending waiting time; do not let it dry on the surface.

Scrape off the paint when it begins to bubble, using a putty knife. Rinse the stripped surfaces with water and dry them with a clean rag. Strip the paint on the remaining box surfaces and repeat as needed in stubborn areas.

VARIATION: As an alternative to stripping the paint, you can sand it off with a grinder or rotary tool with a sanding disc. Sanding also works well for removing paint from stubborn areas after using paint stripper (after the stripper is cleaned from the surface). Wear a respirator when sanding to prevent inhaling paint dust.

DRILLING HOLES IN METAL

Drilling metal is easy but requires some special techniques. Most standard drill bits are designed for both wood and metal and should work well as long as they're sharp. Follow these tips for easy, clean holes in metal:

- Use a slow drill speed. High drill speed is good for wood but bad for metal; it overheats the bit and quickly dulls it. So keep the drill speed low and steady.
- Apply even, light-to-moderate pressure on the bit. Let the drill bit do the work. If you see smoke, you're pressing too hard and/or drilling too fast.
- Add oil, if desired. When drilling holes in thick metal, it helps to lubricate the bit and metal with a few drops of multi-purpose or household oil. Often this isn't necessary with thin metals (such as a toolbox), but it can help when it's taking a while for the bit to get through.
- Drill a pilot hole, if desired. When drilling large holes (over ¼" or so), it can be difficult to get the bit started. Often it helps to drill a smaller pilot hole first, using a ⅛" or smaller bit. The pilot hole gives the larger bit an edge to bite into, so it starts cutting right away. Sometimes it helps to use multiple, progressively larger pilot holes, but with thin metal, one pilot hole usually works best.
- Clean up the edges. Drilling metal usually leaves a rough edge or sharp burrs around the edge of the hole on one or both sides of the metal. If a hole won't be covered by hardware, smooth any rough edges with a metal file, sandpaper, or a grinder or rotary tool with a sanding disc.

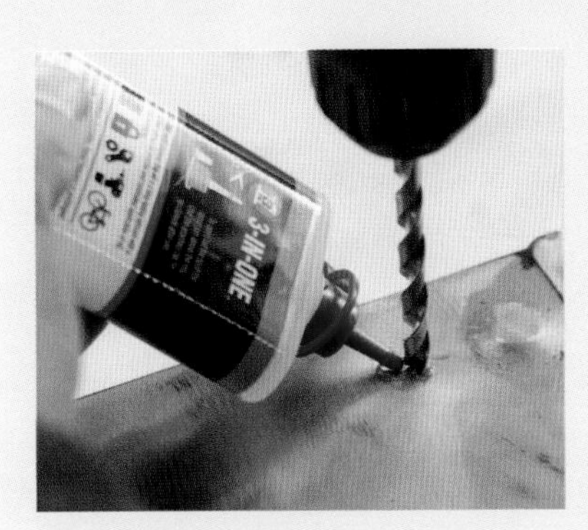

Oil helps keep down the heat when holes are taking a while to drill. Remember: Slow and steady wins the race.

Pilot holes help when large bits have a hard time getting started.

File or sand any edges that will be exposed in the finished project.

(continued)

Drill the ventilation holes.

Drill the ventilation holes. These are optional and can be omitted, resized, or moved as desired. The holes shown are ½" in diameter and located ½" from the bottom edge of the toolbox. There are three holes at each end, located at 2" and 4" from the front and rear sides of the box. Drill the holes with a drill-driver and one or more drill bits; see **Drilling Holes in Metal** on page 151. File or sand the edges of the holes; they will be exposed.

WARNING: Always wear safety glasses when drilling metal.

Mark the holes for the four bolt—two on each end—that will support the coal grate. Locate these close to the ventilation holes. Drill the holes with a ¼" bit.

Create the four holes for the legs. The legs are ½" bolts that should extend at least 2½" below the bottom of the toolbox. You can have taller legs, if desired, by simply using longer bolts. Locate the legs so they are centered about 1" from the front/rear sides and ends of the box, adjusting the location as needed to avoid supports or reinforced joints on the box. Drill the holes, starting with a ⅛" pilot hole and finishing with a ½" bit.

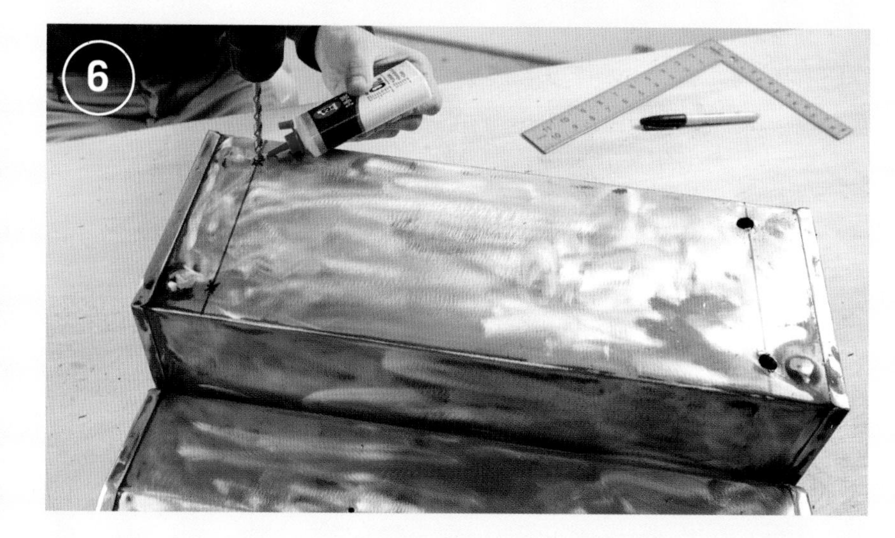

Locate the two handles for carrying the grill and the single handle for the lid. The carrying handles can go in any convenient location as long as they don't interfere with the cooking grate. If the handles are 6½" long (as shown), the handle bolts should be about 5" apart. The lid handle should be centered on the lid. If there is existing hardware from the old handle, the bolts for the new handle can go outside (toward the box ends) of the hardware, and you can make this handle as long as needed. Drill the holes for the handle bolts with a ¼" bit.

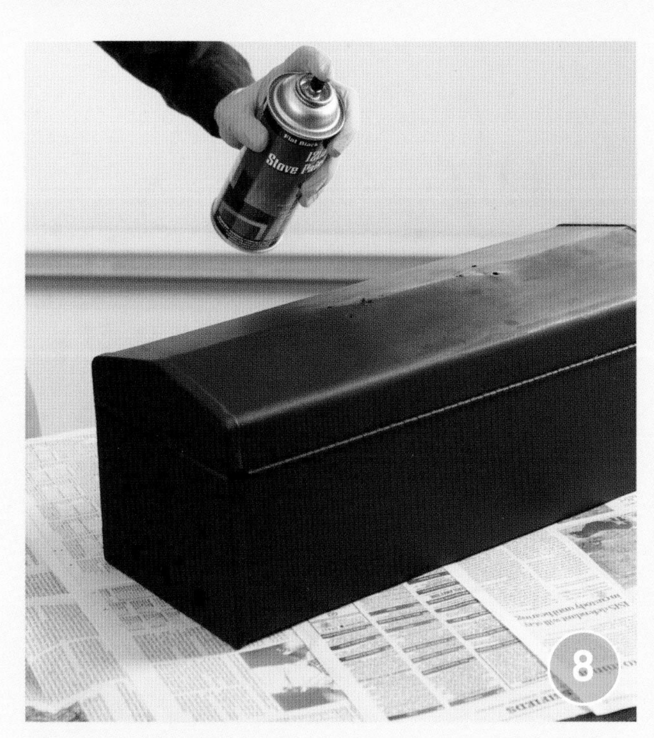

Paint the outside of the box with high-temp spray paint. Apply the paint as directed by the manufacturer. Painting with three or more very thin coats is best to ensure proper adhesion and even coverage and to prevent drips and runs. Let the paint dry between coats, as directed. See **Painting Custom Logos** on page 155 for more painting ideas.

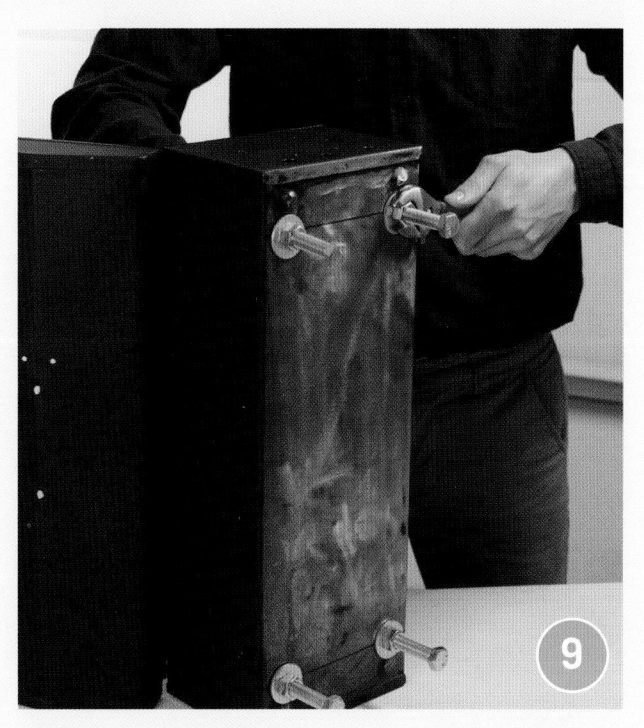

Install ½ × 3" bolts for the legs using two washers and two nuts. Thread a nut onto each bolt so it is about 1" from the end. Add a washer and insert the bolt end through the bottom of the box so the head of the bolt is pointing down. Add another washer and a nut threaded on loosely. Make sure the box stands level on all four legs, adjusting the lower nut as needed to raise or lower each leg. When the box is level, tighten the upper nut on each leg with an adjustable wrench while holding the lower nut in place with a second wrench. *(continued)*

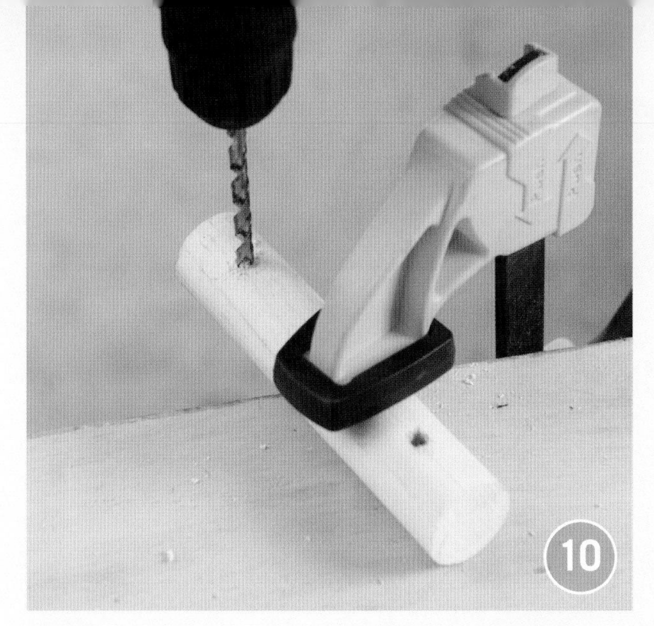

Create the handles. Cut three lengths of 1¼" wood dowel to length, using a jigsaw or handsaw. The handles should be about 1½" longer than the distance between the centers of the handle bolt holes in the box (as shown, the bolt holes are 5" apart; the handles are 6½" long). Mark the two bolt holes onto each handle to match the corresponding holes in the box. Drill a counterbore hole at each mark; the hole should be slightly larger and deeper than the width and height of the bolt head, respectively. At the center of each counterbore, drill a ¼" hole entirely through the handle. Sand the handle smooth with sandpaper.

Install the handles with ¼ × 2¾" carriage bolts. Insert the bolts through the outside of each handle so the bolt head fits into the counterbore. Add a washer and nut on the inside of the handle, leaving the nuts loose for now. Add another washer and nut at the end of each bolt. Insert the bolts into the pair of holes in the box and secure them on the inside of the box with another washer and nut (each bolt gets three washers and nuts). Tighten the bolts against the box wall, then tighten the nuts against the handle.

Cut the coal grate from expanded metal sheet so it fits the bottom of your toolbox. The grate should be as large as possible but small enough that it's easy to get into and out of the box. You will need to remove it to clean out the ash on the box bottom. Cut the grate with a jigsaw with a metal-cutting blade or with heavy-duty metal snips. File the cut edges of the grate to remove sharp edges and points.

WARNING: Wear safety glasses and heavy gloves when cutting and handling metal sheets; cut edges can be extremely sharp.

Install ¼ × 1" stove bolts onto the box for supporting the coal grate, using a washer and nut on the inside of the box. The threaded ends of the bolts will protrude about ⅝" into the box interior. Set the coal grate onto the threaded ends of the bolts.

Fit a cooking grate into the grill. We used an adjustable replacement grill, but you could also cut a piece of expanded metal similar to the coal grate. Do not use grate material that is not designed for grilling, such as wire shelving, as it may contain a coating that is not heat-proof and may emit toxic fumes or degrade under high temperatures. File any sharp edges of the grate. Place the grate into the box, on top of the tray supports.

NOTE: If your box does not have tray supports, install four ¼ × 1" stove bolts (same as the coal-grate supports) to support the cooking grate.

PAINTING CUSTOM LOGOS

Tailgating is all about your team and, of course, grilling. Put the two together by painting your grill or other equipment with your team's logo.

1. Find an image of your logo online, or create your own, and print it out full-size onto standard printer paper. If the image is too big for one page, print onto multiple pages and cut and tape the pieces together.
2. Cut out the logo from the paper to create a template, using a craft knife. Use a ruler as a straightedge for cutting clean, straight lines. Freehand any curved lines. Trim some of the excess paper surrounding the logo, if necessary, to fit the template on your grill.
3. Hold the template in place on the grill and secure it with a few small pieces of masking tape.
4. Tape over the entire of the logo with masking tape. Overlap the parallel strips of tape to ensure there are no gaps between strips.
5. Cut along the outline of the logo with a craft knife, leaving only the logo image in tape. Burnish the edges of the tape with your fingernail to make sure the tape is fully adhered.
6. Paint the box with multiple thin coats of spray paint, as directed by the manufacturer. Let the paint dry between coats.
7. Peel off the masking tape after the final coat of paint has dried, revealing your logo.

Trailer Hitch Table

Of all the items on a tailgating equipment checklist, one of the most difficult to find is a good, solid, convenient work surface. You can use a folding table, but most of these, especially portable, lightweight versions, are flimsy and unstable, and they can blow over if a wind picks up. If you have a truck, you can use the tailgate itself, but these aren't designed as tables and have very little flat space (as you're reminded every time you set down a drink in the wrong place on your tailgate).

The Trailer Hitch Table solves this problem with a perfectly simple solution: a table that mounts to your trailer hitch. It's sizable, flat, and sturdy, and it assembles and disassembles in less than a minute. Best of all, the table surface rotates 360° so you can set it up just how you like it—for food prep, grilling, serving, eating, or just for gathering around for drinks.

There are two key parts to this project: the trailer hitch post, which supports the table, and the floor flange, which connects the tabletop to the post. These parts are easy to find online, but you have to get the right sizes so they're a good fit for each other and for your vehicle's trailer hitch. The hitch post shown here has a square end that's sized for a standard 2-inch receiver hitch. The other end of the post is round and measures 2⅜ inches diameter. The round end of the post is essential for giving the table full rotation. The post shown here also can accept a picnic-style grill, which is designed to fit onto a vertical post.

The floor flange is a galvanized steel fitting designed for mounting chain-link fence posts to concrete surfaces. It has a round socket that fits over the end of the hitch post. The inner diameter of the socket is 2½ inches. The socket has two setscrew bolts that you can snug up to the post to secure the tabletop in any position.

TOOLS & MATERIALS

- Circular saw
- Weights
- Jigsaw with fine-tooth wood blade (optional)
- Sanding block or power sander
- Framing square
- Drill-driver and 3⁄16" drill bit
- 9⁄16" or 14mm socket and driver or socket wrench
- Adjustable wrench
- ¾ × 48 × 48" exterior-grade plywood
- Waterproof wood glue
- 80-, 150-, and 220-grit sandpaper
- Paint or other finish and related supplies
- Eye and ear protection
- Work gloves

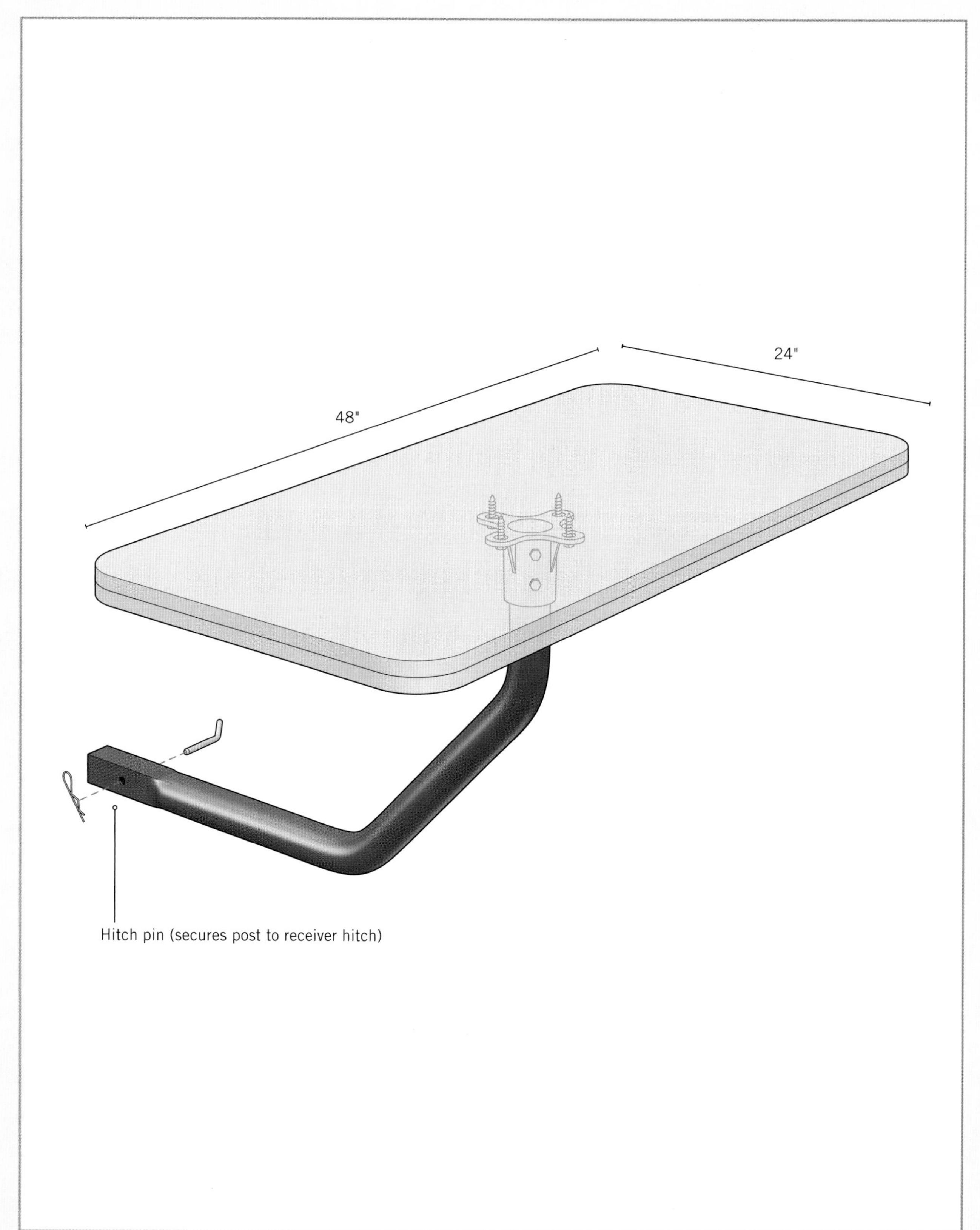
24"
48"
Hitch pin (secures post to receiver hitch)

TRAILER HITCH TABLE

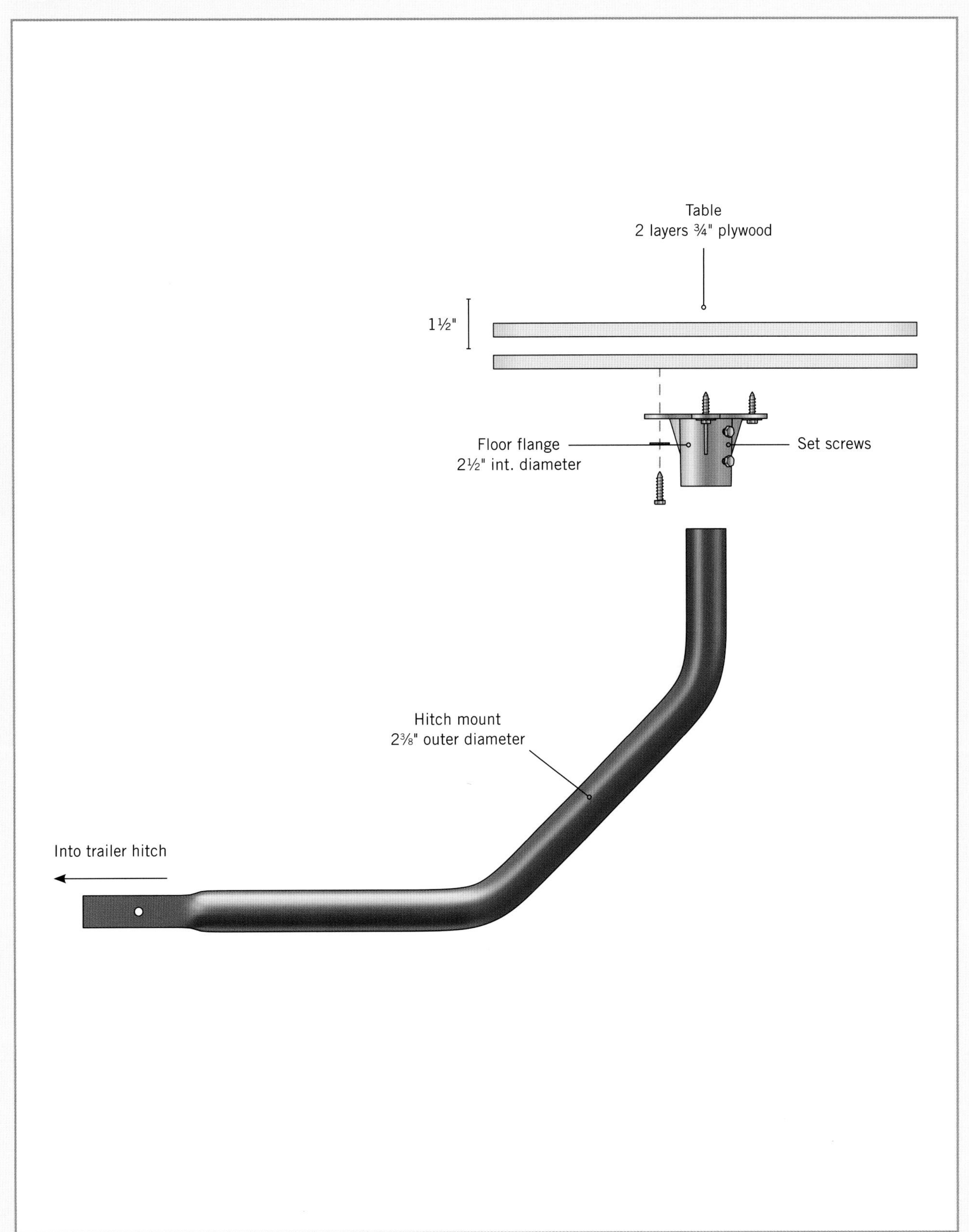

How to Build the Trailer Hitch Table

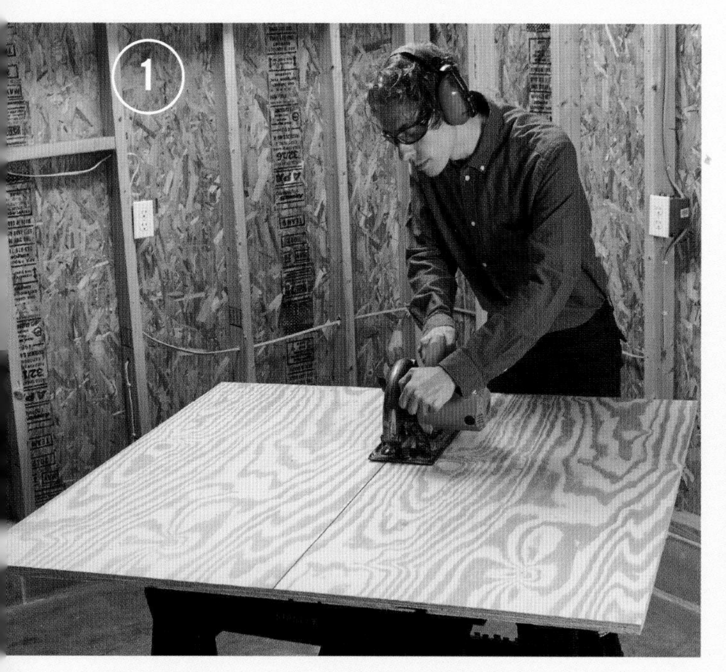

Cut the two layers of the tabletop to size at 24 × 48" or as desired, using a circular saw. If you're using a half-sheet (4 × 4') of plywood, make the cut precisely down the middle of the sheet so the two halves are the same size.

Apply thin, wavy beads of waterproof wood glue to the top face of one of the plywood pieces. Make sure there is a continuous bead about ½" from all edges.

Place the other piece of plywood onto the glued surface and press it down firmly. Align the edge of the two pieces, then weight down the top piece with several heavy weights. Let the glue dry for 24 hours, then remove the weights.

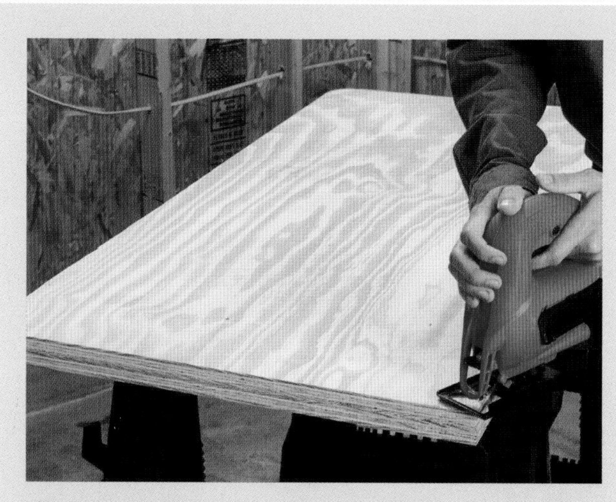

OPTION: Create curved corners on the table by tracing along the edge of a compact disc (CD) or other round object and cutting the corners with a jigsaw.

TIP: To minimize splintering on the plywood surface, use a fine-tooth wood blade and move the saw slowly. Also, set the orbital action on the saw to "0" so the blade cuts straight up and down, not with an elliptical motion.

Sand the edges of the table with 80- or 100-grit sandpaper so they are flat and smooth, using a sanding block or power sander. Sand the edges again with 150-grit sandpaper, then sand the edges and the table faces with 220-grit so everything is smooth to the touch.

Finish the tabletop as desired. The simplest option is to paint it or give it a clear coat of polyurethane, but you can customize either of those treatments with a logo. Or, you can cover the top and edges with plastic laminate for the ideal food-prep surface. See **Choose Your Table Surface** on page 163.

Place the tabletop face down on a covered work surface (to protect the finish). Mark the center of the tabletop along the width and length, making a small cross at its center. Use a framing square set against the table's edges to extend the marks about 4" from the center, creating 8"-long lines that cross in the center.

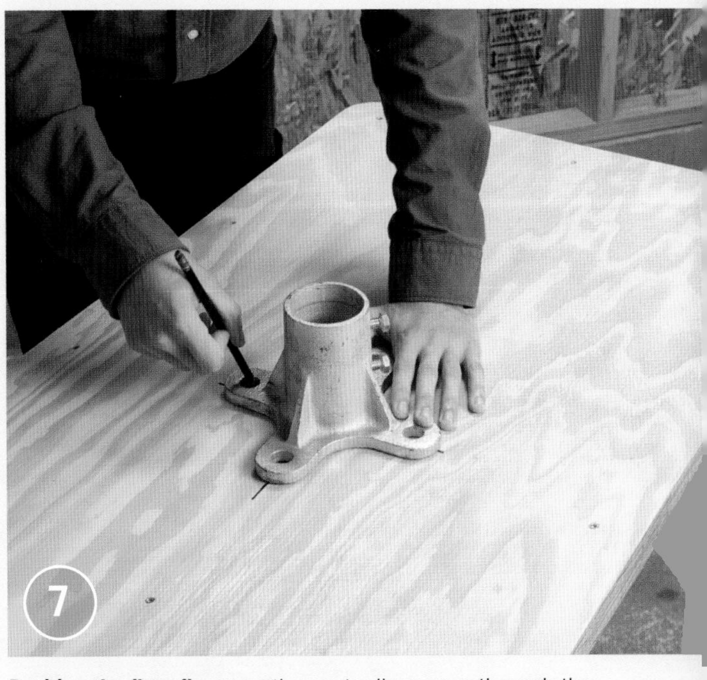

Position the floor flange so the center lines pass through the centers of the flange's mounting holes. Mark the center of each hole, then remove the flange. Drill a 3⁄16" hole at each mark, drilling no more than 1¼" deep.

(continued)

Mount the floor flange to the bottom of the tabletop with four ⅜ × 1¼" lag screws, using a 9⁄16" or 14mm socket and drill-driver or socket wrench. Tighten the screws snug, but be careful not to overtighten them, which could strip the pilot holes.

Set up the table by fitting the lower end of the hitch mount into a 2" receiver hitch on your vehicle and securing the mount with a hitch pin (the pin typically is not sold with this type of mount). Place the tabletop onto the upper end of the hitch mount, fitting the floor flange over the end of the mount. Rotate the table to the desired position, then lock it in place by tightening the two setscrew bolts on the floor flange, using an adjustable wrench or socket wrench.

OPTION: The trailer hitch mount used in this project also works with a picnic-style grill, which is made to mount onto a post. The grill must have a post-fitting underneath that fits a 2⅜" (outer diameter, O.D.) post. Like the tabletop, the grill can be rotated to any convenient position and can be secured with a bolt or hitch pin.

CHOOSE YOUR TABLE SURFACE

The best thing about building your own tailgate table is that you can customize it to fit right into your setup. Do you want team colors or logos? Natural wood? Or maybe a real countertop material? Follow these tips for the best results.

Paint: Use a high-gloss enamel for a durable, washable surface. Apply the paint with a foam roller for smooth finishes. It's best to paint all of the surfaces, including the underside, for moisture protection and to prevent warping.

If you want to include a custom logo, you can paint the logo area in one color and let it dry. Use the template technique described on page 155, applying tape over the painted area. However, use blue painter's tape instead of masking tape because painter's won't stick to the paint. Paint the rest of the table in a different color, then peel off the tape to reveal your logo. Alternatively, you can have the logo image be bare wood, then seal over it with clear lacquer or polyurethane.

Clear finish: For a natural-wood look, use exterior polyurethane or spar varnish, which is designed for outdoor projects. Apply three coats to all surfaces for a smooth, durable finish.

Laminate: Plastic laminate—the countertop material—makes for the ultimate food-prep surface and is surprisingly easy to apply with small projects. You can buy 30"-wide sheets of laminate in a range of colors (standard sheets are 60" wide). You'll also need a router or laminate trimmer with a flush-trimming laminate bit.

To apply laminate, cut the edge pieces so they are about ½" wider and longer than each table edge. This is a rough cut and can be made with a circular saw, jigsaw, or even tin snips. Apply contact cement to one of the table edges and to the backside of the laminate strip. Let the cement dry, as directed. Press the laminate onto the table edge, then roll the surface with a J-roller to make sure it's fully adhered. Trim the excess laminate flush to the table edges with the router or laminate trimmer.

Repeat the same process to cover the remaining table edges, then the top. The magic of the laminate bit is that it cuts flush to the wood table surface or the previously installed laminate without damaging it. When the top surface is laminated, use a fine metal file to smooth all of the trimmed edges and corners of the laminate. Hold the file at steep angle and move it parallel to the edge. This step is essential because trimmed laminate is razor-sharp before it is filed.

Pub Table Cooler

The Pub Table Cooler has you covered for the two most essential items for any outdoor party: iced beverages and a place to hang out (and set down your drinks). Somebody should have thought of this a long time ago.

Here's how the project works: The cooler is a standard galvanized steel tub, the kind you can buy at any hardware store (or may already own). The tub gets a plywood base underneath its bottom to add rigidity and help support the table. On the inside of the tub bottom, you mount a floor flange, a round, galvanized steel base with a threaded socket at its center. The table leg, or post, is a prethreaded galvanized steel pipe; it threads into the floor flange.

The tabletop is a disc of ¾-inch plywood with a slightly smaller disc of ½-inch plywood underneath, giving the tabletop some weight. (You can also use ¾-inch plywood for both discs.) Another floor flange is mounted to the bottom of the tabletop, and the whole thing screws onto the top threaded end of the leg pipe. When the table is disassembled for travel-mode, the wood top serves as a lid for the cooler tub.

All of the parts for this project are available at any home center or well-stocked hardware store. Floor flanges and pre-threaded pipe are standard plumbing supplies and are designed to fit together. Just make sure to use galvanized pipe and not black steel pipe, which is not rust-resistant. The tub in the project shown here is a 15-gallon size and measures about 22 inches diameter (across the top) and about 11 inches tall. This size is a good compromise between capacity and portability. You can use a different size of tub, but it must be large enough to support the table, and it shouldn't be so large that it weighs a ton when it's full of ice.

TOOLS & MATERIALS

- Wooden yardstick (or similar flat, straight stick)
- Drill-driver
- 1⁄16", ⅛", and ¼" drill bits
- Hammer
- Finish nail ×2
- Pencil (standard or mechanical)
- Jigsaw with fine-tooth wood blade
- Sanding block or power sander
- Weights
- Caulking gun
- Straightedge
- Square
- Screwdriver
- Adjustable wrench
- Eye and ear protection
- Work gloves
- Waterproof wood glue
- 15-gallon galvanized steel tub (1)
- 2 × 4' sheet of ¾" exterior plywood (1)
- 2 × 2' sheet of ½" exterior plywood (1)
- 80- and 150-grit sandpaper
- Rubbing alcohol
- Rags
- Silicone caulk (clear)
- Paint (or other wood/metal finish) and painting supplies
- 1" galvanized steel floor flanges (w/ female threads for 1" galvanized pipe) (2)
- 1 × 36" galvanized steel pipe with prethreaded ends (outside diameter approx. 1¼") (1)
- 1½" galvanized coarse-thread wood screws (4)
- ¼ × 1½" galvanized or stainless-steel flathead machine bolts, with washers and nuts (4)

PUB TABLE COOLER

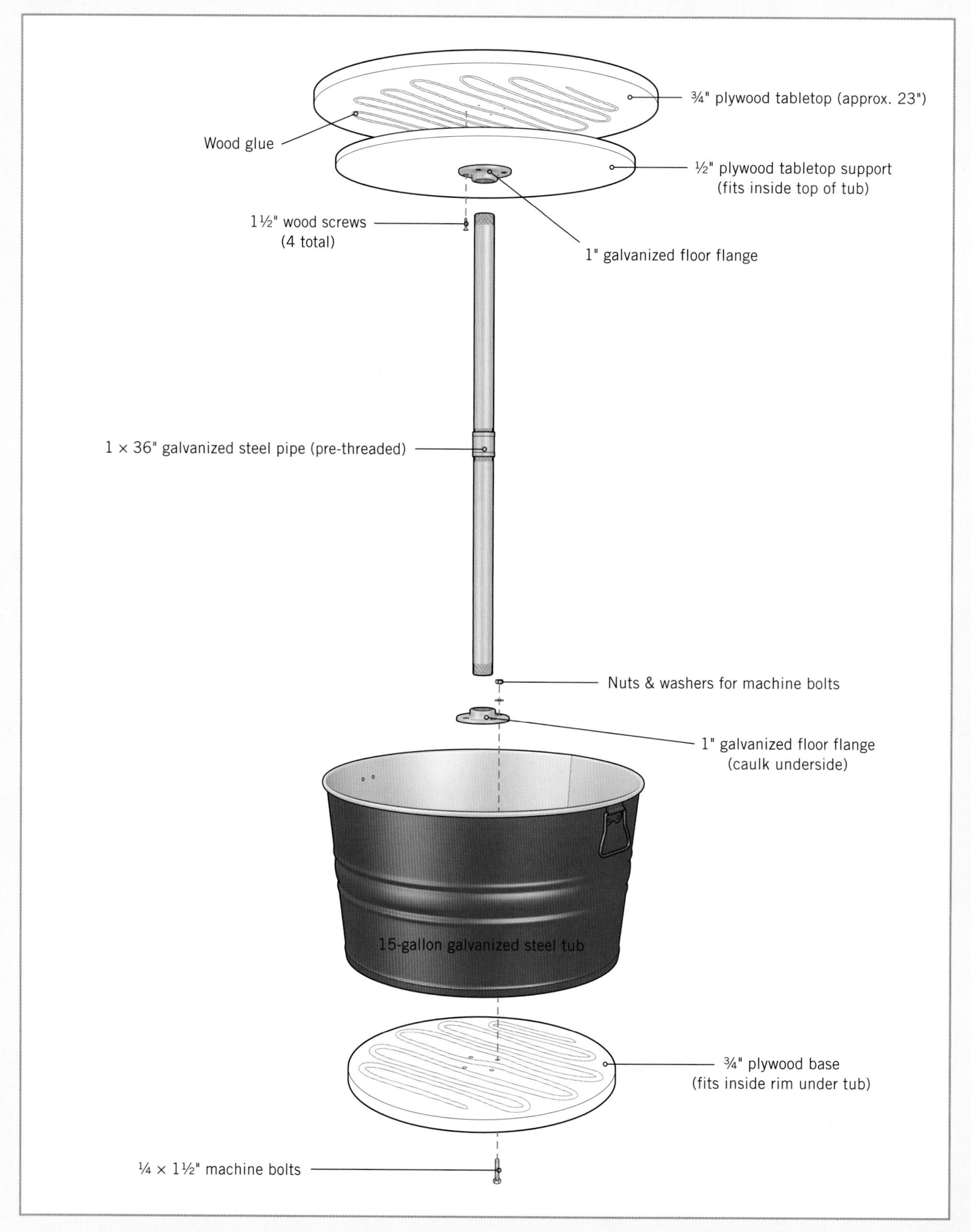

How to Build the Pub Table Cooler

Measure the diameter of the tub for the three plywood discs: the base, the tabletop support, and the tabletop. For the base, measure inside the lip or edge on the bottom of the tub, then subtract ¼"; the base will sit inside the lip. For the tabletop support, measure the inside diameter at the top rim of the tub, then subtract ⅛"; the support should fit snugly inside the rim. For the tabletop, measure the outside diameter of the rim, then add ½". Convert all three dimensions to a radius by dividing each by 2. For example, if the outside of the tub measures 22", you add ½" = 22½". Divide by 2 = 11¼". The radius of the tabletop is 11¼".

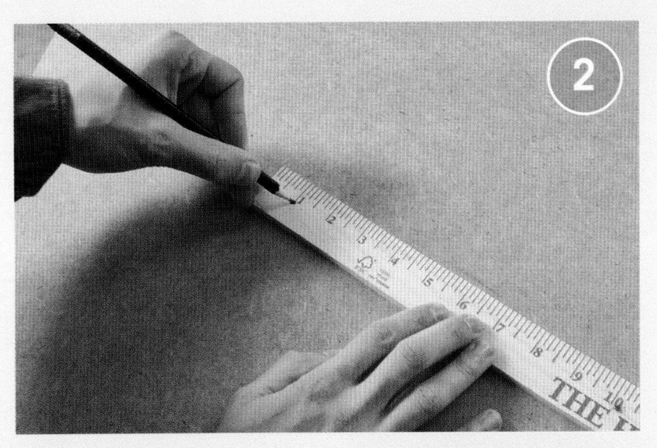

Create a trammel for drawing the three circles onto plywood. Drill a 1/16" hole at the center of a wooden yardstick, about 1" from the end. This hole is for a finish nail that serves as the trammel's pivot point. Measure from the hole, and mark the stick, using the radius dimensions calculated for the base, tabletop support, and tabletop. Drill a 1/16" or ⅛" hole at each mark; these are for inserting a pencil to draw the circles.

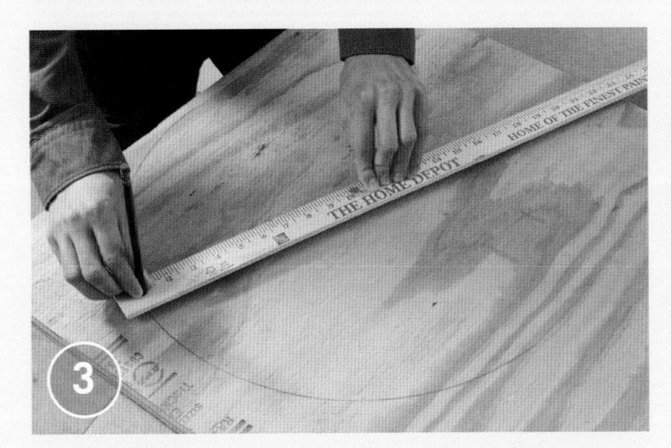

Place the trammel onto a piece of ¾" plywood so the circle (when drawn) will be close to two of the plywood's edges (to conserve material). Drive a small finish nail through the 1/16" hole and partway into the plywood to fix the trammel at the pivot point. Insert the point of a pencil into the hole for the tabletop radius. Rotate the trammel and pencil through a full circle to draw a cutting line for the tabletop. Repeat the process to draw the base on the ¾" plywood. Draw the tabletop support on a piece ½" plywood. Optionally, you can use ¾" plywood for all three pieces.

TIP: Designate the face of each piece with the nail hole as the bottom so you can easily find the center of the disc later.

Cut out the three plywood discs using a jigsaw.

TIP: To minimize splintering on the plywood surface, use a fine-tooth wood blade and move the saw slowly. Also, set the orbital action on the saw to "0" so the blade cuts straight up and down, not with an elliptical motion. Sand the edges of the pieces with 80-grit sandpaper and a sanding block or power sander so the curved edges are smooth and consistent. Sand all of the surfaces with 150-grit sandpaper.

(continued)

Apply a wavy bead of waterproof wood glue to the top face of the tabletop support. Place the tabletop disc face-up on a flat surface, and place the glued face of the support onto the tabletop so it is perfectly centered. Add heavy weights to the support to compress the pieces evenly. Let the glue dry overnight, then remove the weights.

Clean the bottom (outside) of the tub with soap and water, then wipe it with rubbing alcohol and a rag to remove any residue from the metal surface. Apply a thick, wavy bead of silicone caulk to the top face of the plywood base. Set the tub onto the base and weight it down evenly inside the tub. Let the caulk cure overnight, then remove the weights.

Paint the tabletop and/or the tub as desired. If you're using the table for tailgating, this is a great opportunity to show your team colors or add a custom logo (see **Painting Custom Logos** on page 155). Use high-gloss enamel paint for the table, and use spray paint for the tub. If you prefer a natural wood finish, give the table a clear coat of exterior polyurethane or spar varnish, follow the manufacturer's directions.

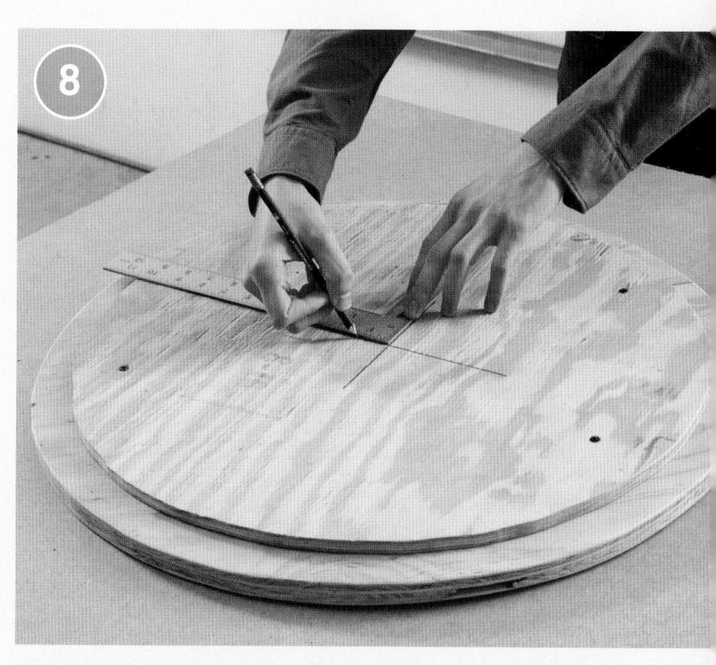

Draw a line across the center of the tabletop support and the base, using a straightedge aligned with the nail hole from the trammel. Use a square to draw a perpendicular line through the first line, also aligned with the center hole.

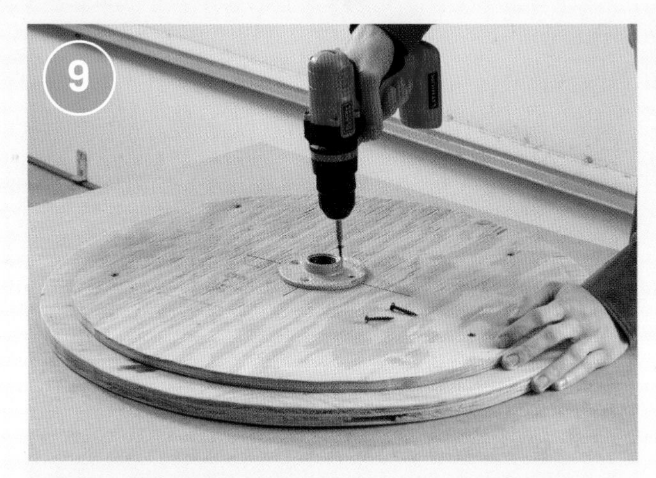

Position a floor flange onto the bottom face of the tabletop support so the flange's mounting holes are centered over the lines. Trace inside the holes to mark their locations. Remove the flange, and drill a ⅛" pilot hole at each location, drilling no more than 1¼" deep so you don't drill through the tabletop surface. Mount the floor flange to the tabletop support with 1½" wood screws.

Mark the mounting holes for the other floor flange onto the bottom face of the plywood base piece. Drill ¼" holes through the base and the bottom of the tub. Insert a ¼ × 1½" machine bolt through the base and into the bottom of the tub. Apply a heavy bead of silicone caulk along the perimeter on the underside of the floor flange. Set the floor flange into the tub, aligning it with the bolts. Secure the flange to the bolts with washers and nuts, and tighten them with a screwdriver and adjustable wrench. Let the caulk cure for 24 hours.

USING THE PUB TABLE COOLER

Once the caulk has fully cured (typically 24 hours), your table is ready for use. To set up the table, thread a 1 × 36" galvanized steel plumbing pipe into the floor flange inside the tub. Hand-tighten the pipe.

Position the tabletop (with attached floor flange) onto the top end of the pipe and rotate the table clockwise to thread the flange onto the pipe. Turn the top carefully at first to make sure the threads are seated; misalignment, or cross-threading, will ruin the threads on the pipe or the flange.

Fill the tub with ice and beverages, and you're open for business! When the party's over, simply unscrew the tabletop and pipe. Dump out any excess water from the tub, then cover it with the tabletop for the ride home.

Metric Conversions

ENGLISH TO METRIC

TO CONVERT:	TO:	MULTIPLY BY:
Inches	Millimeters	25.4
Inches	Centimeters	2.54
Feet	Meters	0.305
Yards	Meters	0.914
Square inches	Square centimeters	6.45
Square feet	Square meters	0.093
Square yards	Square meters	0.836
Ounces	Milliliters	30.0
Pints (US)	Liters	0.473 (Imp. 0.568)
Quarts (US)	Liters	0.946 (Imp. 1.136)
Gallons (US)	Liters	3.785 (Imp. 4.546)
Ounces	Grams	28.4
Pounds	Kilograms	0.454

TO CONVERT:	TO:	MULTIPLY BY:
Millimeters	Inches	0.039
Centimeters	Inches	0.394
Meters	Feet	3.28
Meters	Yards	1.09
Square centimeters	Square inches	0.155
Square meters	Square feet	10.8
Square meters	Square yards	1.2
Milliliters	Ounces	.033
Liters	Pints (US)	2.114 (Imp. 1.76)
Liters	Quarts (US)	1.057 (Imp. 0.88)
Liters	Gallons (US)	0.264 (Imp. 0.22)
Grams	Ounces	0.035
Kilograms	Pounds	2.2

LUMBER DIMENSIONS

NOMINAL - U.S.	ACTUAL - U.S. (IN INCHES)	METRIC
1 × 2	¾ × 1½	19 × 38 mm
1 × 3	¾ × 2½	19 × 64 mm
1 × 4	¾ × 3½	19 × 89 mm
1 × 5	¾ × 4½	19 × 114 mm
1 × 6	¾ × 5½	19 × 140 mm
1 × 7	¾ × 6¼	19 × 159 mm
1 × 8	¾ × 7¼	19 × 184 mm
1 × 10	¾ × 9¼	19 × 235 mm
1 × 12	¾ × 11¼	19 × 286 mm
1¼ × 4	1 × 3½	25 × 89 mm
1¼ × 6	1 × 5½	25 × 140 mm
1¼ × 8	1 × 7¼	25 × 184 mm
1¼ × 10	1 × 9¼	25 × 235 mm
1¼ × 12	1 × 11¼	25 × 286 mm
1½ × 4	1¼ × 3½	32 × 89 mm
1½ × 6	1¼ × 5½	32 × 140 mm
1½ × 8	1¼ × 7¼	32 × 184 mm
1½ × 10	1¼ × 9¼	32 × 235 mm
1½ × 12	1¼ × 11¼	32 × 286 mm
2 × 4	1½ × 3½	38 × 89 mm
2 × 6	1½ × 5½	38 × 140 mm
2 × 8	1½ × 7¼	38 × 184 mm
2 × 10	1½ × 9¼	38 × 235 mm
2 × 12	1½ × 11¼	38 × 286 mm
3 × 6	2½ × 5½	64 × 140 mm
4 × 4	3½ × 3½	89 × 89 mm
4 × 6	3½ × 5½	89 × 140 mm

CONVERTING TEMPERATURES

Convert degrees Fahrenheit (F) to degrees Celsius (C) by following this simple formula: Subtract 32 from the Fahrenheit temperature reading. Then multiply that number by 5⁄9. For example, 77°F - 32 = 45. 45 × 5⁄9 = 25°C.

To convert degrees Celsius to degrees Fahrenheit, multiply the Celsius temperature reading by 9⁄5. Then, add 32. For example, 25°C × 9⁄5 = 45. 45 + 32 = 77°F.

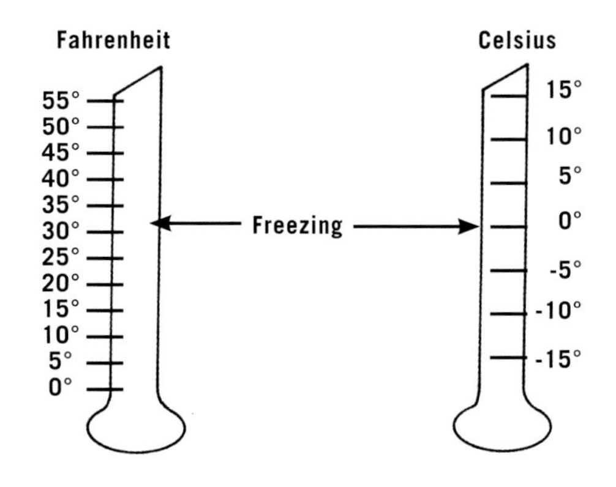

LIQUID MEASUREMENT EQUIVALENTS

1 Pint	= 16 Fluid Ounces	= 2 Cups
1 Quart	= 32 Fluid Ounces	= 2 Pints
1 Gallon	= 128 Fluid Ounces	= 4 Quarts

METRIC PLYWOOD PANELS

Metric plywood panels are commonly available in two sizes: 1,200 mm × 2,400 mm and 1,220 mm × 2,400 mm, which is roughly equivalent to a 4 × 8' sheet. Standard and Select sheathing panels come in standard thicknesses, while Sanded grade panels are available in special thicknesses.

STANDARD SHEATHING GRADE		SANDED GRADE	
7.5 mm	(5/16")	6 mm	(4/17")
9.5 mm	(3/8")	8 mm	(5/16")
12.5 mm	(1/2")	11 mm	(7/16")
15.5 mm	(5/8")	14 mm	(9/16")
18.5 mm	(3/4")	17 mm	(2/3 ")
20.5 mm	(13/16")	19 mm	(3/4")
22.5 mm	(7/8")	21 mm	(13/16")
25.5 mm	(1")	24 mm	(15/16")

COUNTERBORE, SHANK & PILOT HOLE DIAMETERS

SCREW SIZE	COUNTERBORE DIAMETER FOR SCREW HEAD (IN INCHES)	CLEARANCE HOLE FOR SCREW SHANK (IN INCHES)	PILOT HOLE DIAMETER	
			HARD WOOD (IN INCHES)	SOFT WOOD (IN INCHES)
#1	.146 (9/64)	5/64	3/64	1/32
#2	1/4	3/32	3/64	1/32
#3	1/4	7/64	1/16	3/64
#4	1/4	1/8	1/16	3/64
#5	1/4	1/8	5/64	1/16
#6	5/16	9/64	3/32	5/64
#7	5/16	5/32	3/32	5/64
#8	3/8	11/64	1/8	3/32
#9	3/8	11/64	1/8	3/32
#10	3/8	3/16	1/8	7/64
#11	1/2	3/16	5/32	9/64
#12	1/2	7/32	9/64	1/8

NAILS

Nail lengths are identified by numbers from 4 to 60 followed by the letter "d," which stands for "penny." For general framing and repair work, use common or box nails. Common nails are best suited to framing work where strength is important. Box nails are smaller in diameter than common nails, which makes them easier to drive and less likely to split wood. Use box nails for light work and thin materials. Most common and box nails have a cement or vinyl coating that improves their holding power.

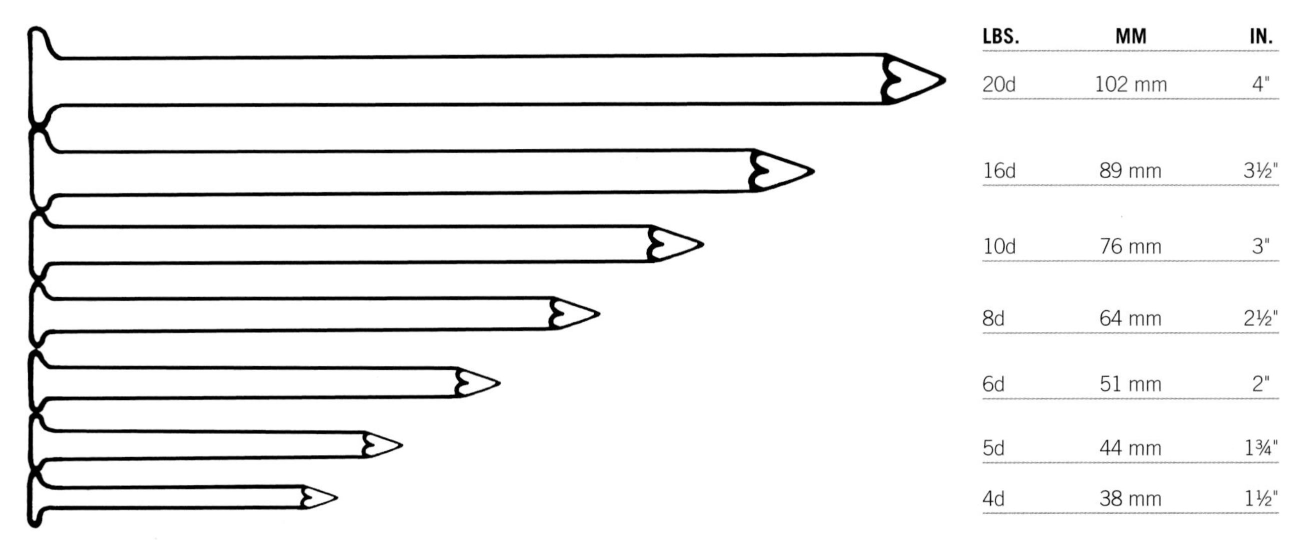

LBS.	MM	IN.
20d	102 mm	4"
16d	89 mm	3½"
10d	76 mm	3"
8d	64 mm	2½"
6d	51 mm	2"
5d	44 mm	1¾"
4d	38 mm	1½"

Resources

A-Maze-N© Smokin' Products, Inc.
1932 Shawnee Road
Eagan, MN 55122
www.amazenproducts.com

Black & Decker (US), Inc.
800 544 6986
www.blackanddecker.com
www.bdk.com

Photo Credits

Shutterstock: 6-22, 24 (left top, left bottom, right bottom), 25, 27 (left), 28 (left), 30-32, 33 (left top, right top), 34-40, 86-88, 136-138

A-Maze-N© Smokin' Products: 28 (right top, right bottom), 33 (right bottom)

Index